GRAPHIC SCIENCE AND ENGINEERING IN ACTION

ENGINEERING AN AWESOME

RECYCLING CENTER

with **MAX AXIOM**
SUPER SCIENTIST

by Nikole Brooks Bethea

illustrated by Pop Art Studios

Consultant:
Morgan Hynes, PhD
Research Assistant Professor, Education
Research Program Manager
Center for Engineering Education and Outreach
Tufts University
Medford, Massachusetts

CAPSTONE PRESS
a capstone imprint

Graphic Library is published by Capstone Press,
1710 Roe Crest Drive, North Mankato, Minnesota 56003
www.capstonepub.com

Library of Congress Cataloging-in-Publication Data
Bethea, Nikole Brooks.
  Engineering an awesome recycling center with Max Axiom, super scientist / by Nikole Brooks
Bethea ; illustrated by Pop Art Studios.
    pages cm.—(Graphic library. Graphic science and engineering in action)
  Includes bibliographical references and index.
  ISBN 978-1-4296-9934-1 (library binding)
  ISBN 978-1-62065-699-0 (paperback)
  ISBN 978-1-4765-1590-8 (ebook PDF)
1. Recycling (Waste, etc.)—Comic books, strips, etc.—Juvenile literature. 2. Recycling center—
Design and construction—Comic books, strips, etc.—Juvenile literature. 3. Graphic novels. I.
Pop Art Studios, illustrator. II. Title.
  TD794.5.B475 2013
  628.4'458—dc23   2012026438

Summary: In graphic novel format, follows Max Axiom as he uses the engineering process to
design and build a recycling center.

Designer
Ted Williams

Production Specialist
Laura Manthe

Cover Illustrator
Marcelo Baez

Editor
Christopher L. Harbo

Media Researcher
Wanda Winch

Printed in the United States   5972

TABLE of CONTENTS

SECTION 1 A GARBAGE PROBLEM

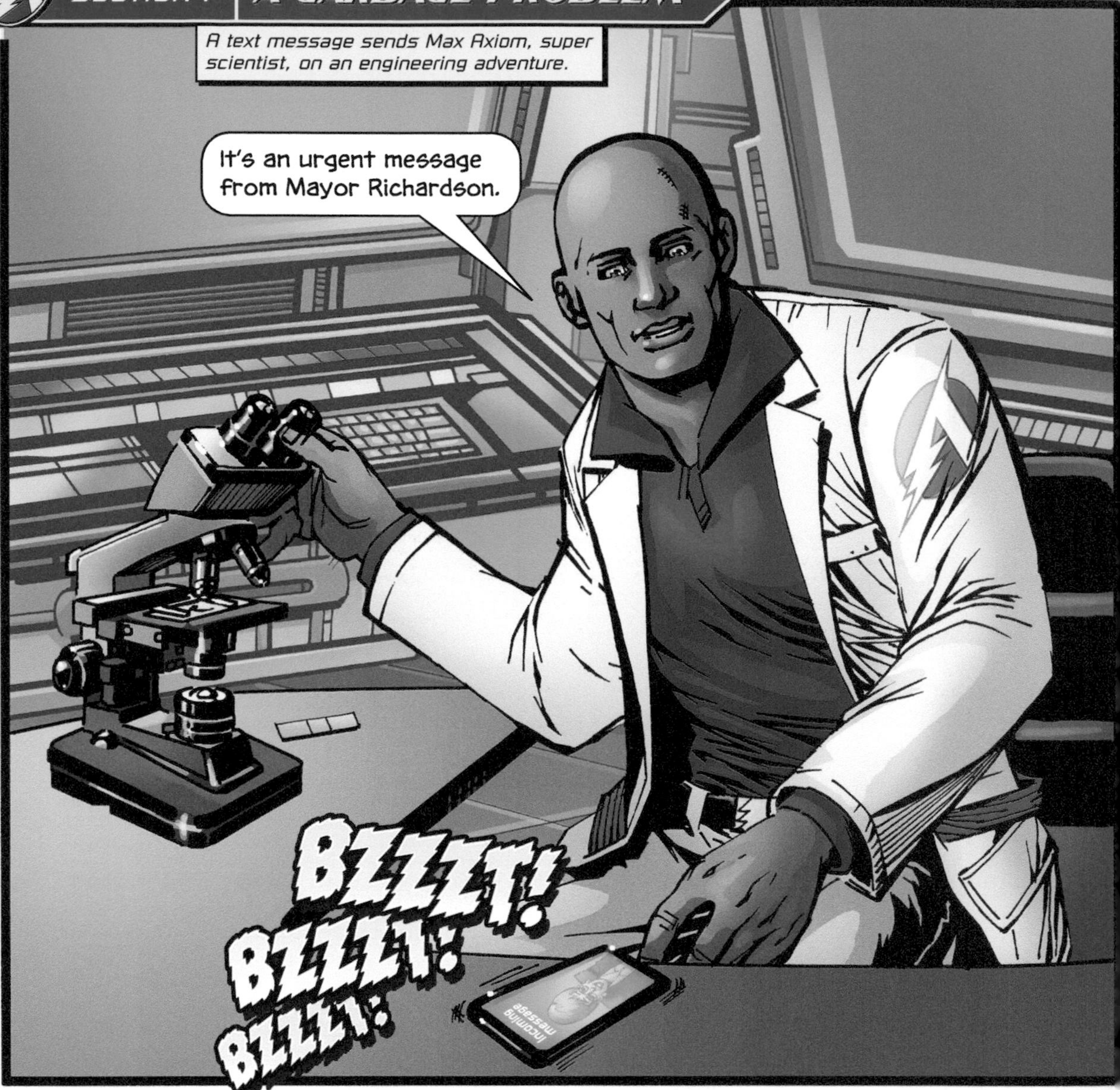

A text message sends Max Axiom, super scientist, on an engineering adventure.
It's an urgent message from Mayor Richardson.
BZZZZT!
BZZZZT!
BZZZZT!
Incoming message

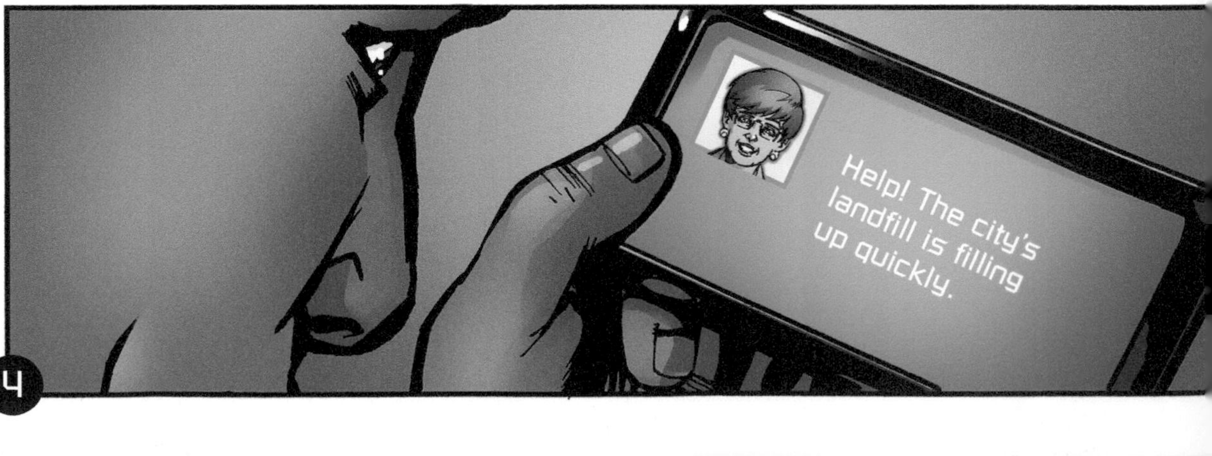

Help! The city's landfill is filling up quickly.

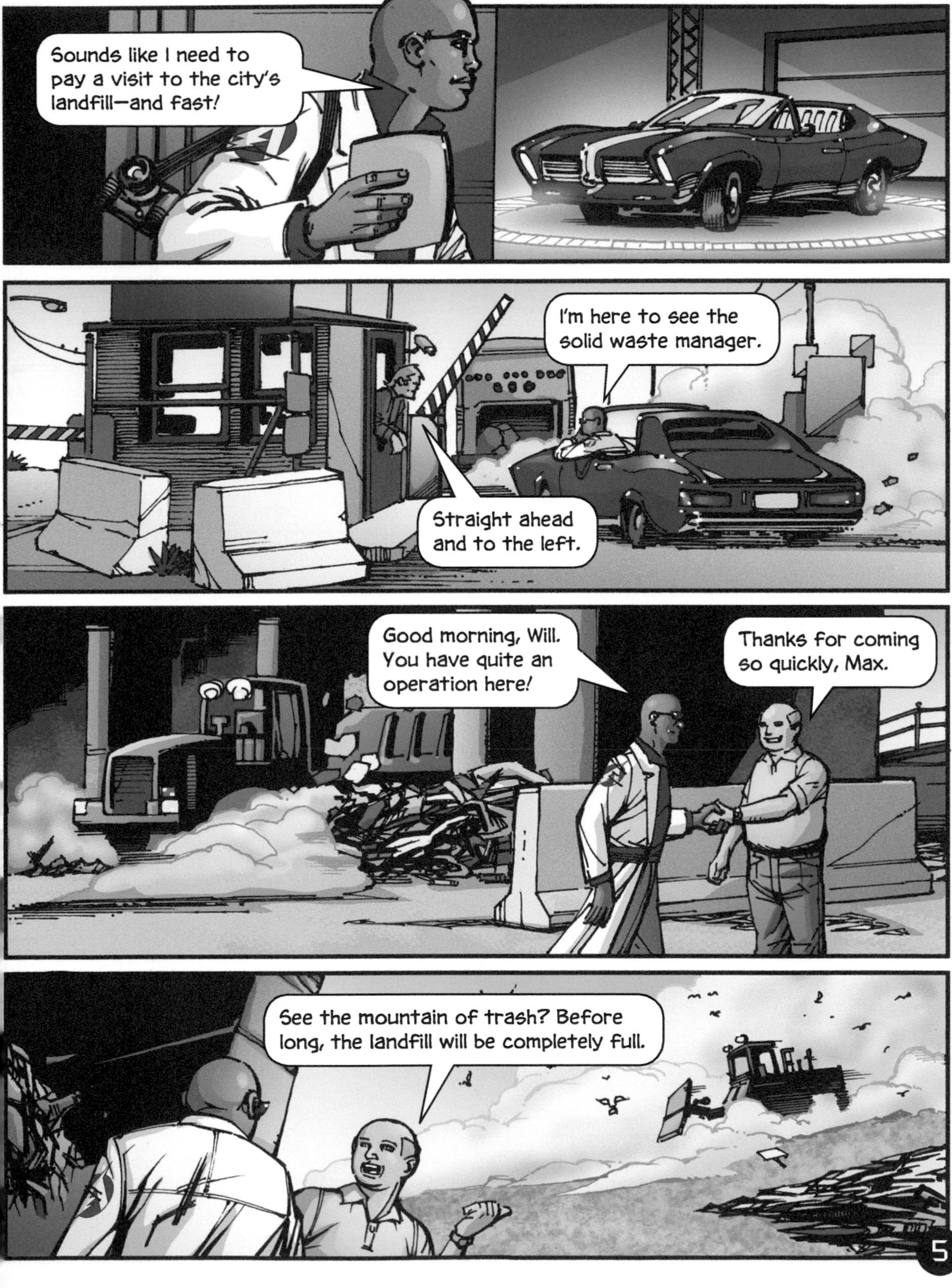
Sounds like I need to pay a visit to the city's landfill—and fast!
I'm here to see the solid waste manager.
Straight ahead and to the left.
Good morning, Will. You have quite an operation here!
Thanks for coming so quickly, Max.
See the mountain of trash? Before long, the landfill will be completely full.

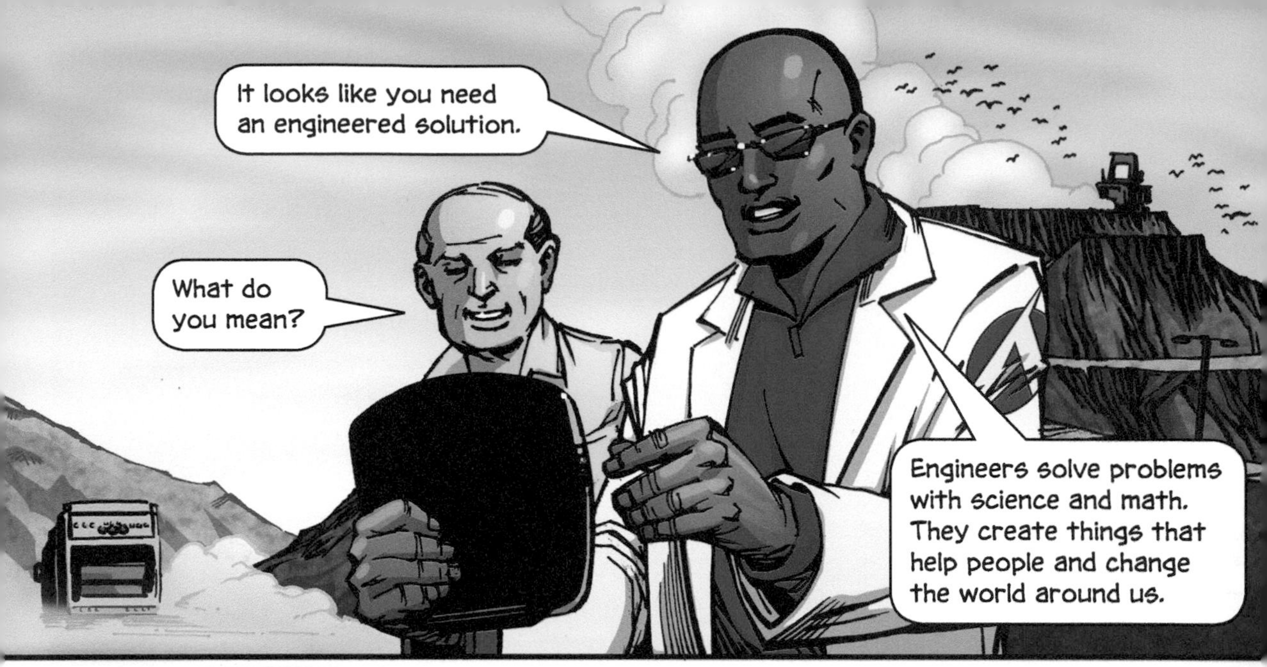
It looks like you need an engineered solution.
What do you mean?
Engineers solve problems with science and math. They create things that help people and change the world around us.

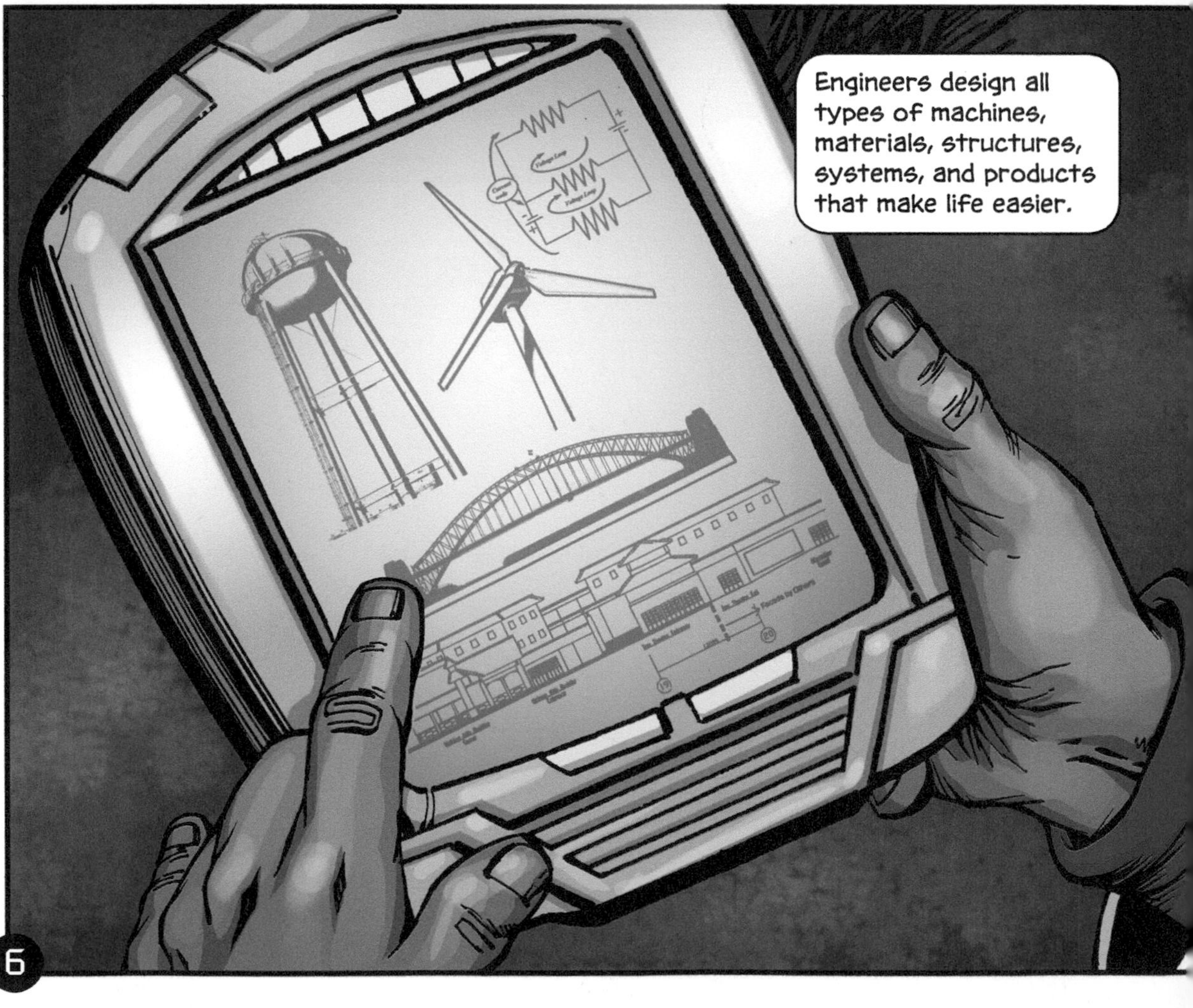
Engineers design all types of machines, materials, structures, systems, and products that make life easier.

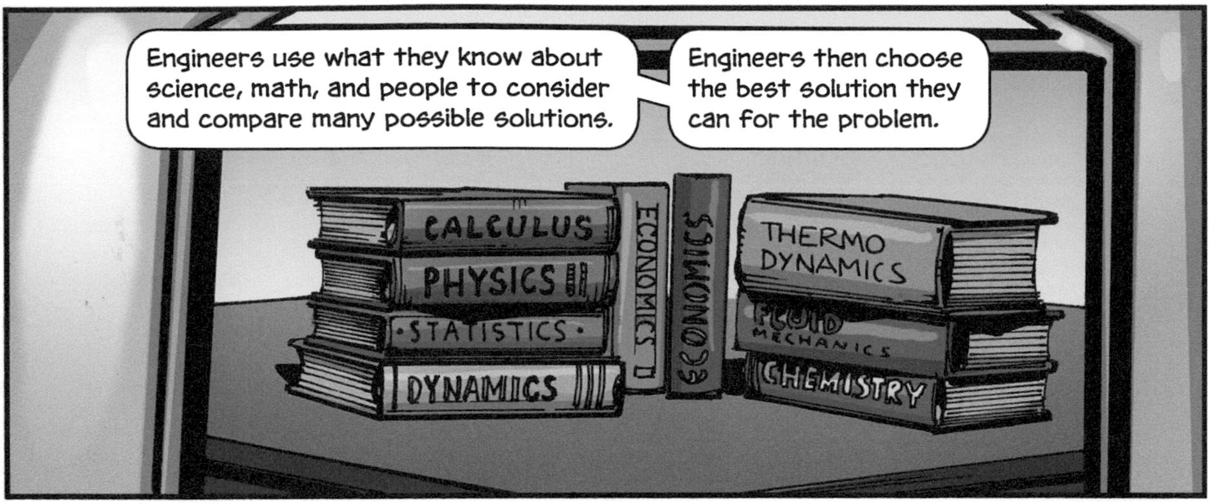
Engineers use what they know about science, math, and people to consider and compare many possible solutions.
Engineers then choose the best solution they can for the problem.
CALCULUS
PHYSICS
STATISTICS
DYNAMICS
ECONOMICS
ECONOMICS
THERMO DYNAMICS
FLUID MECHANICS
CHEMISTRY

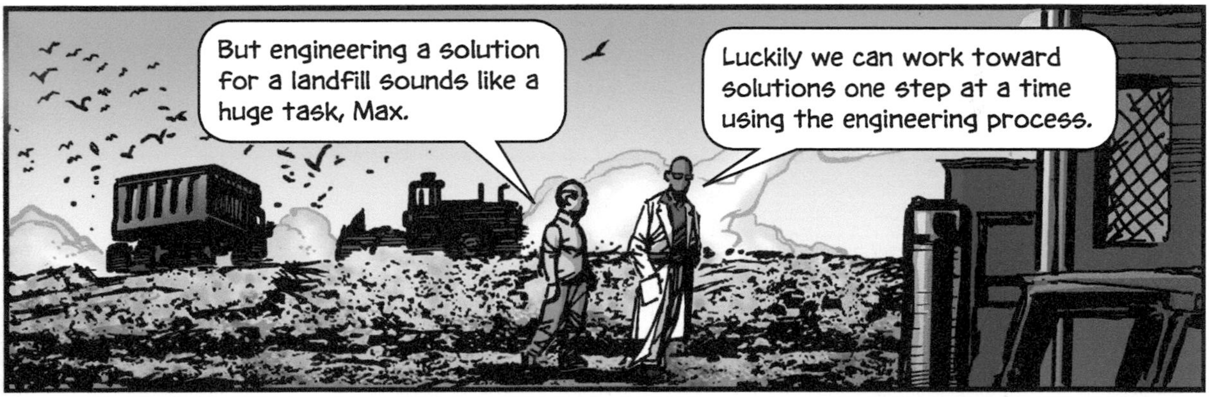
But engineering a solution for a landfill sounds like a huge task, Max.
Luckily we can work toward solutions one step at a time using the engineering process.

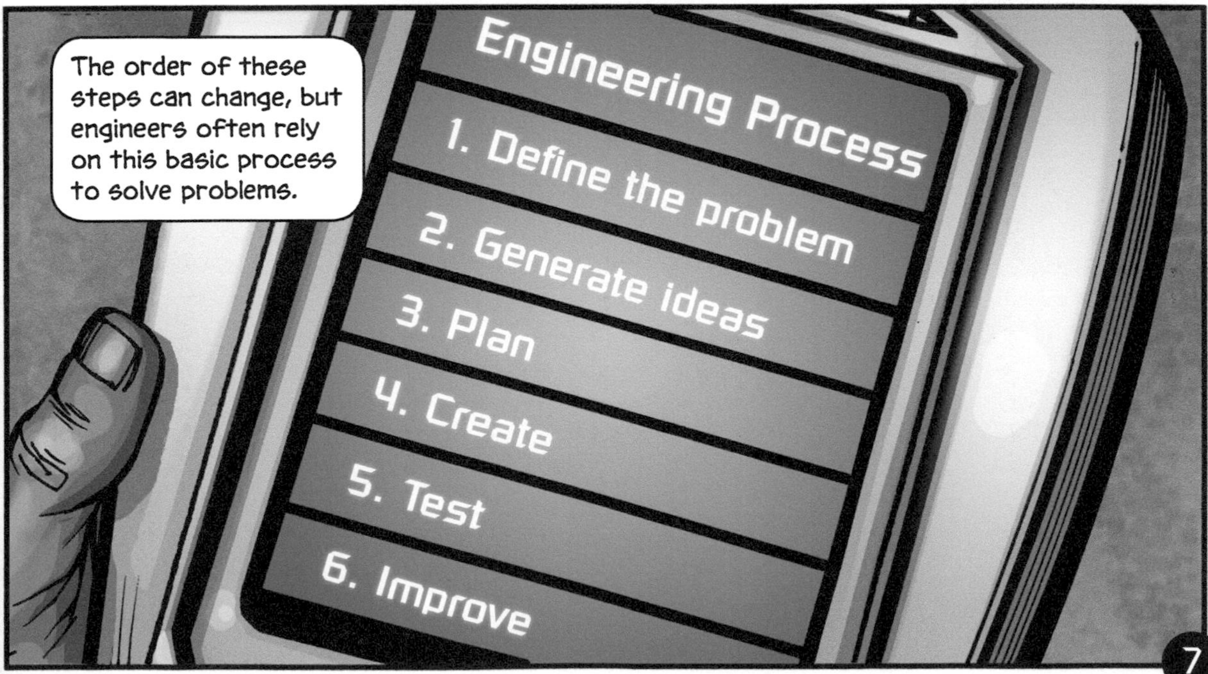
The order of these steps can change, but engineers often rely on this basic process to solve problems.
Engineering Process
1. Define the problem
2. Generate ideas
3. Plan
4. Create
5. Test
6. Improve

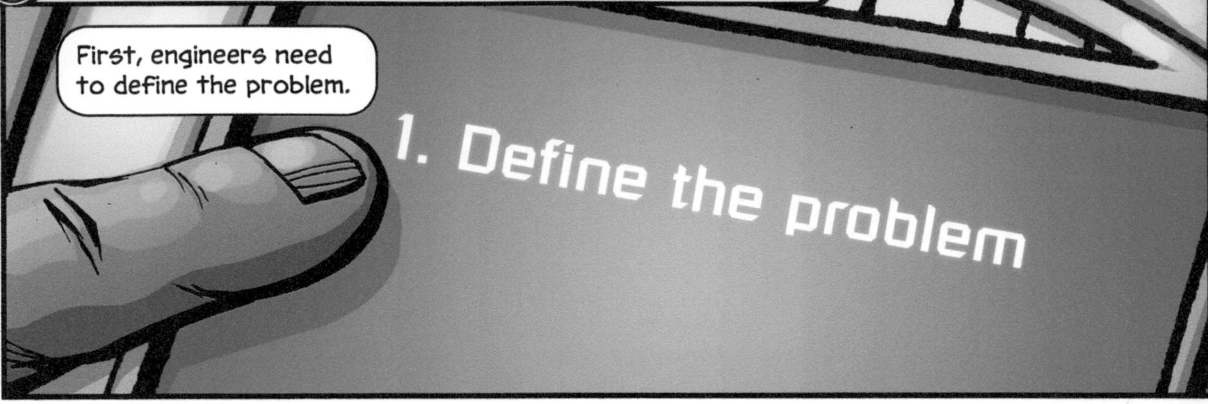
First, engineers need to define the problem.
1. Define the problem

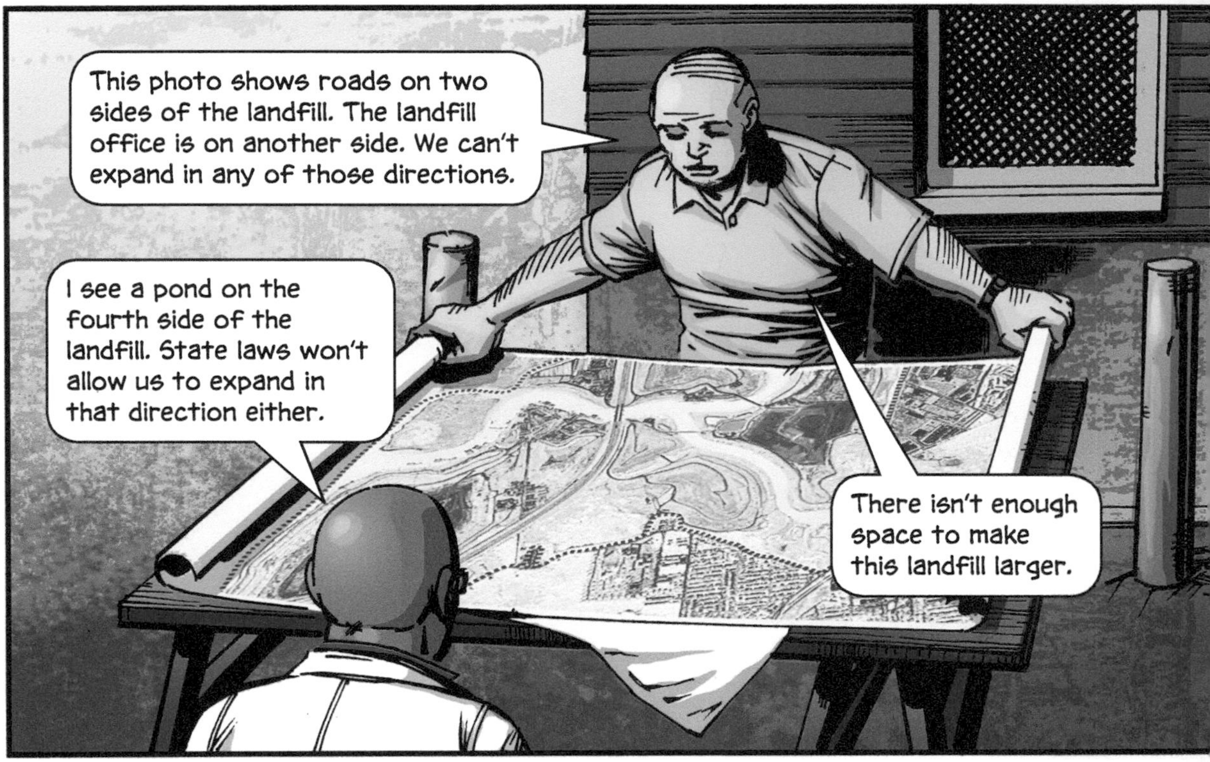
This photo shows roads on two sides of the landfill. The landfill office is on another side. We can't expand in any of those directions.
I see a pond on the fourth side of the landfill. State laws won't allow us to expand in that direction either.
There isn't enough space to make this landfill larger.

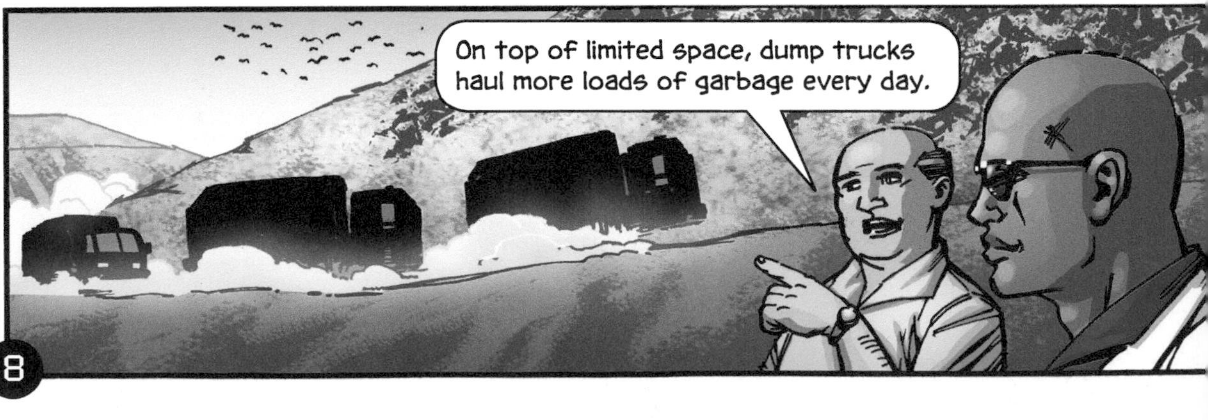
On top of limited space, dump trucks haul more loads of garbage every day.

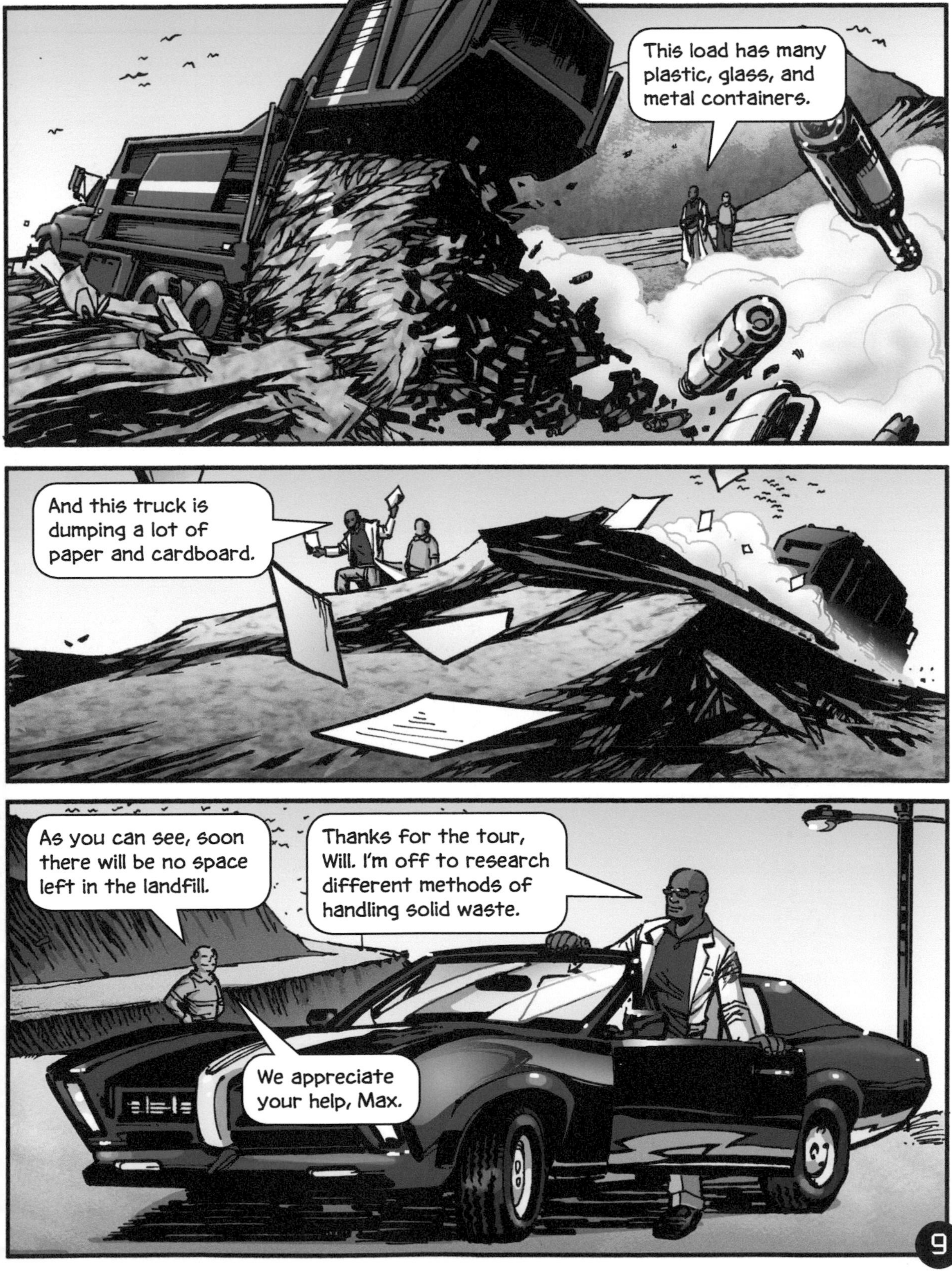
This load has many plastic, glass, and metal containers.
And this truck is dumping a lot of paper and cardboard.
As you can see, soon there will be no space left in the landfill.
Thanks for the tour, Will. I'm off to research different methods of handling solid waste.
We appreciate your help, Max.

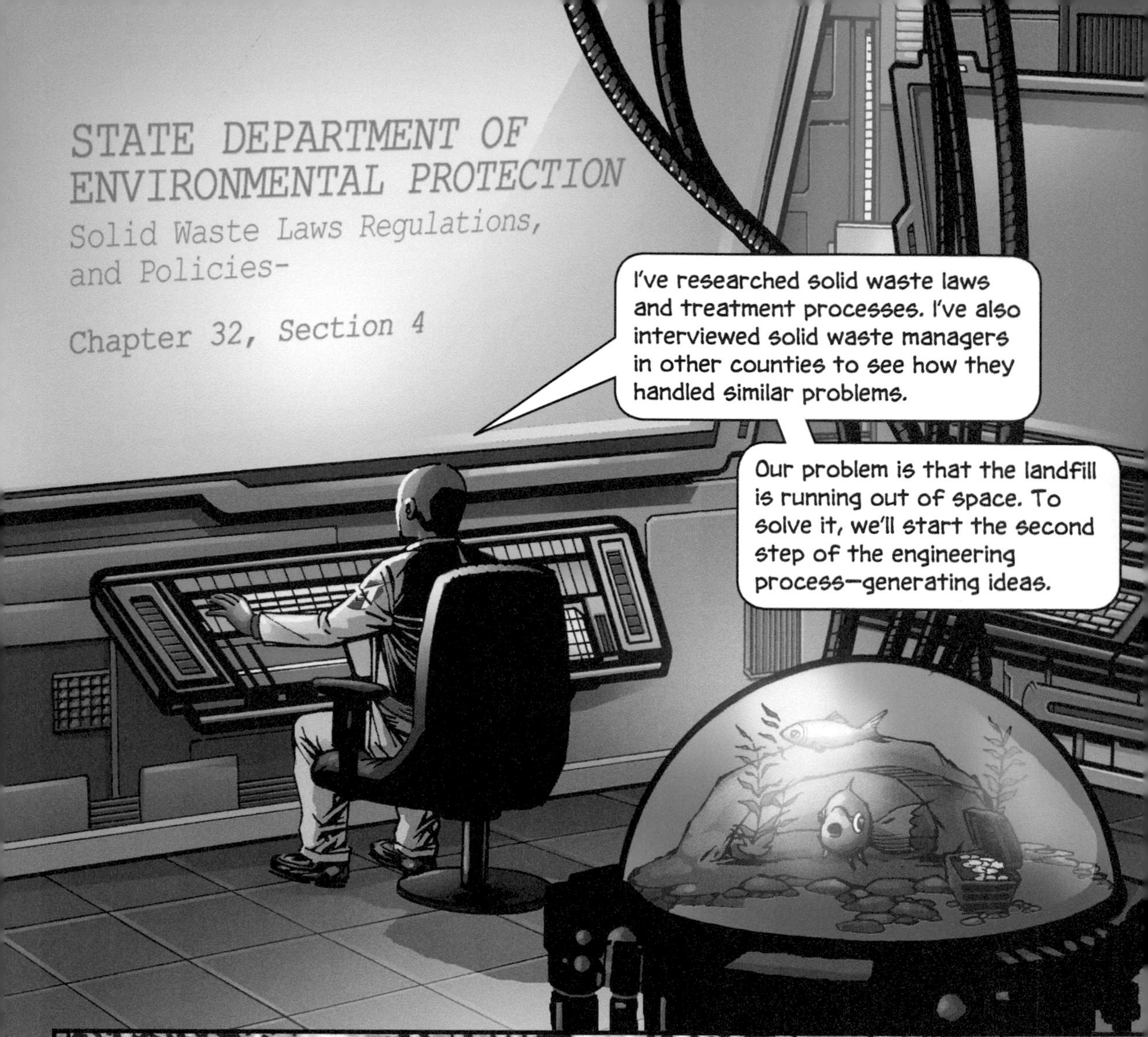
STATE DEPARTMENT OF ENVIRONMENTAL PROTECTION
Solid Waste Laws Regulations, and Policies-
Chapter 32, Section 4
I've researched solid waste laws and treatment processes. I've also interviewed solid waste managers in other counties to see how they handled similar problems.
Our problem is that the landfill is running out of space. To solve it, we'll start the second step of the engineering process—generating ideas.

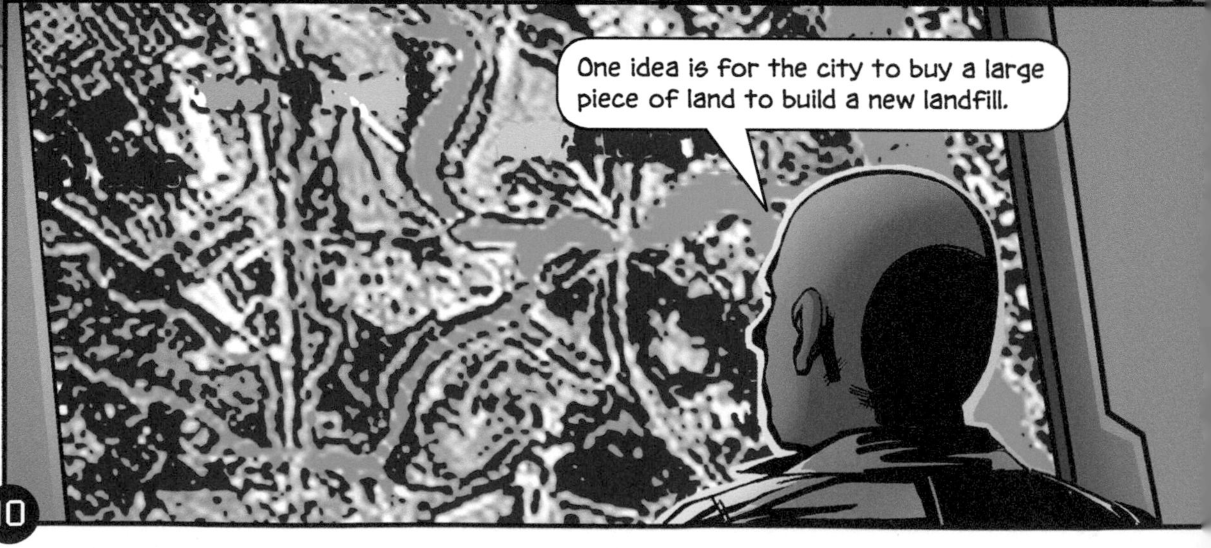
One idea is for the city to buy a large piece of land to build a new landfill.

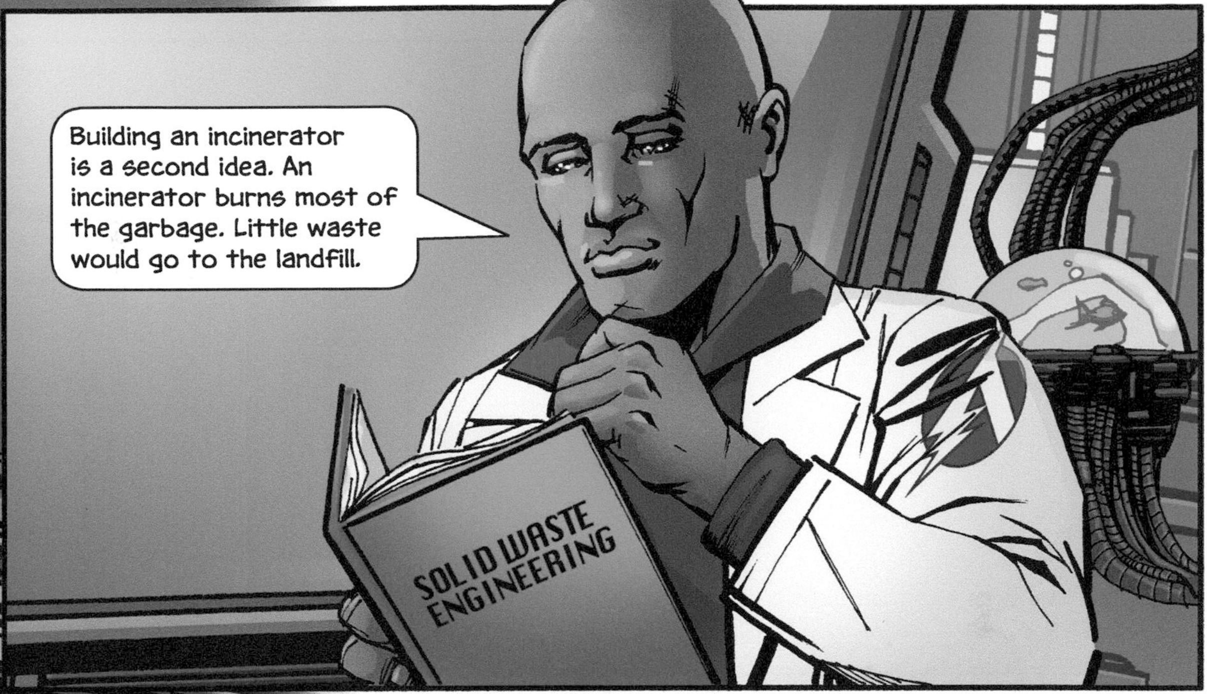
Building an incinerator is a second idea. An incinerator burns most of the garbage. Little waste would go to the landfill.
SOLID WASTE ENGINEERING

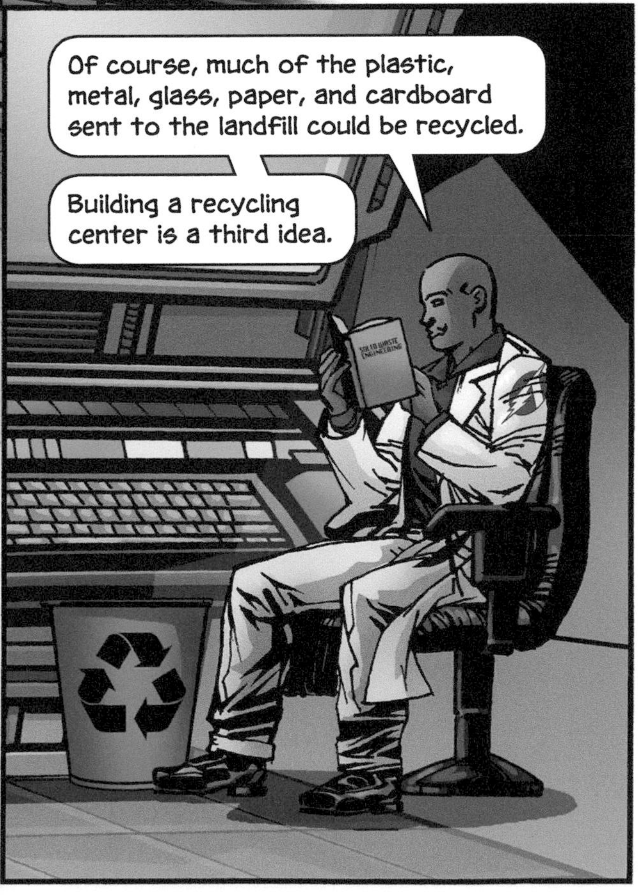
Of course, much of the plastic, metal, glass, paper, and cardboard sent to the landfill could be recycled.
Building a recycling center is a third idea.

GAR-BARGE

In 1987 the *Mobro 4000* barge left New York carrying more than 3,000 tons (2,720 metric tons) of garbage. It traveled 6,000 miles (9,660 kilometers) looking for a place to dispose of the garbage. It was nicknamed the Gar-barge. Six states and three countries turned the barge away. After six months it returned to New York. The garbage was burned at an incinerator. Afterward recycling increased because people were aware of waste disposal issues.

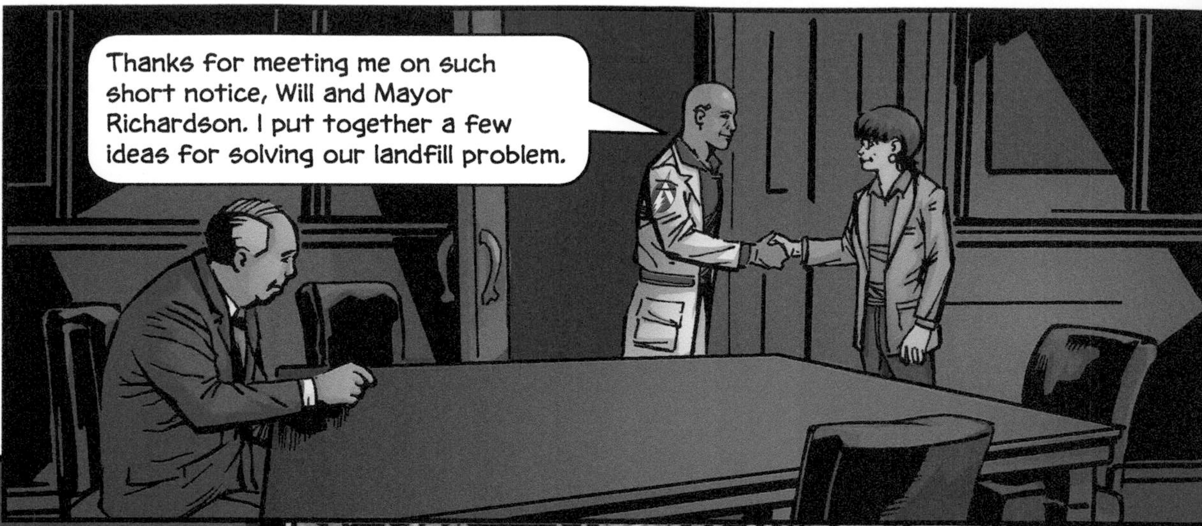
Thanks for meeting me on such short notice, Will and Mayor Richardson. I put together a few ideas for solving our landfill problem.

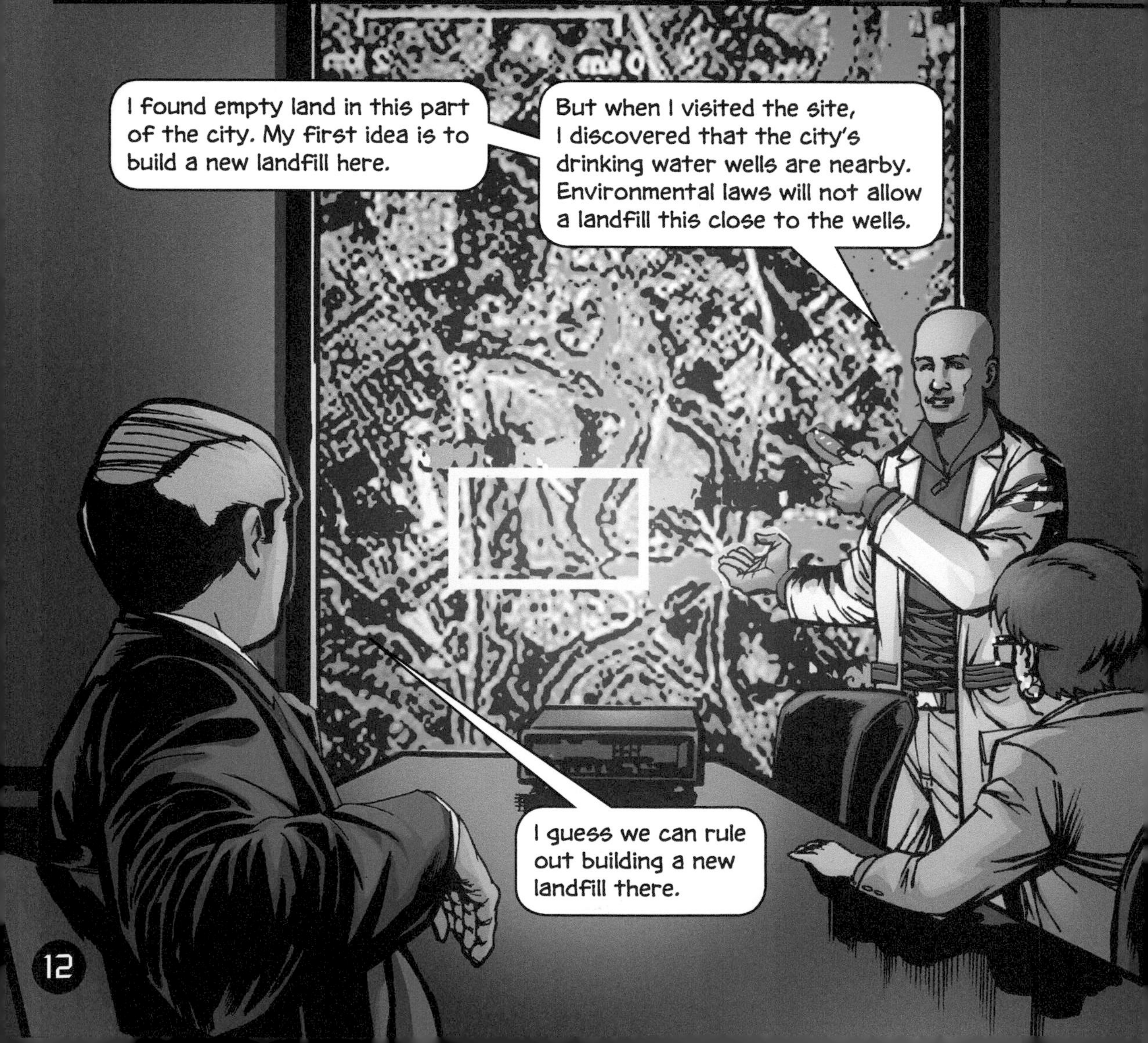
I found empty land in this part of the city. My first idea is to build a new landfill here.
But when I visited the site, I discovered that the city's drinking water wells are nearby. Environmental laws will not allow a landfill this close to the wells.
I guess we can rule out building a new landfill there.

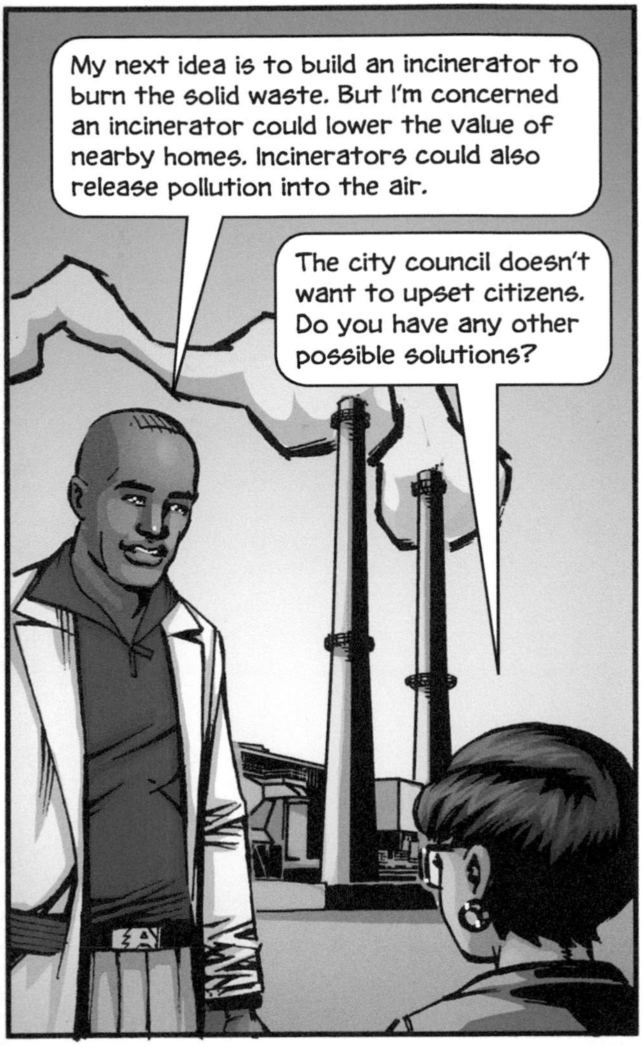
My next idea is to build an incinerator to burn the solid waste. But I'm concerned an incinerator could lower the value of nearby homes. Incinerators could also release pollution into the air.
The city council doesn't want to upset citizens. Do you have any other possible solutions?

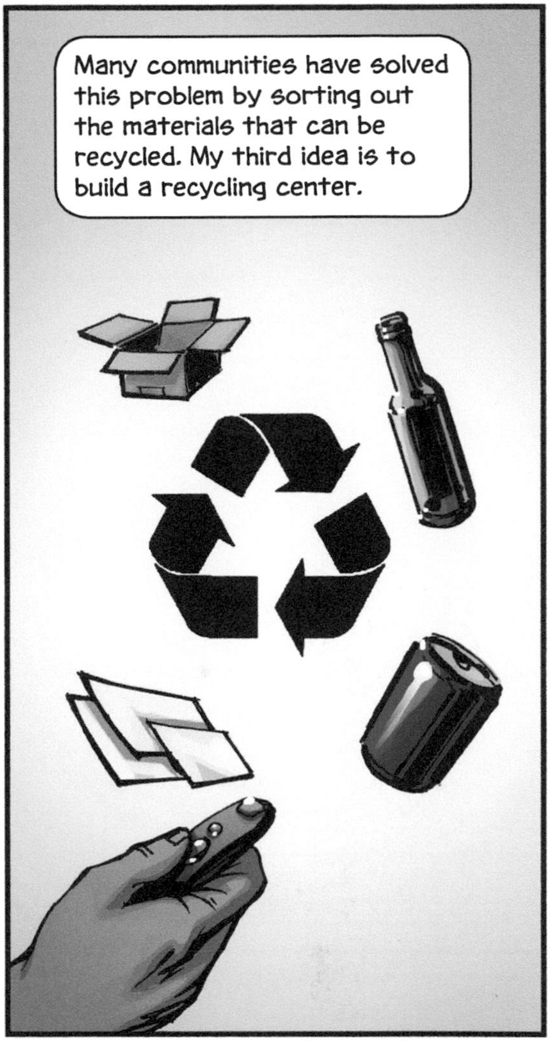
Many communities have solved this problem by sorting out the materials that can be recycled. My third idea is to build a recycling center.

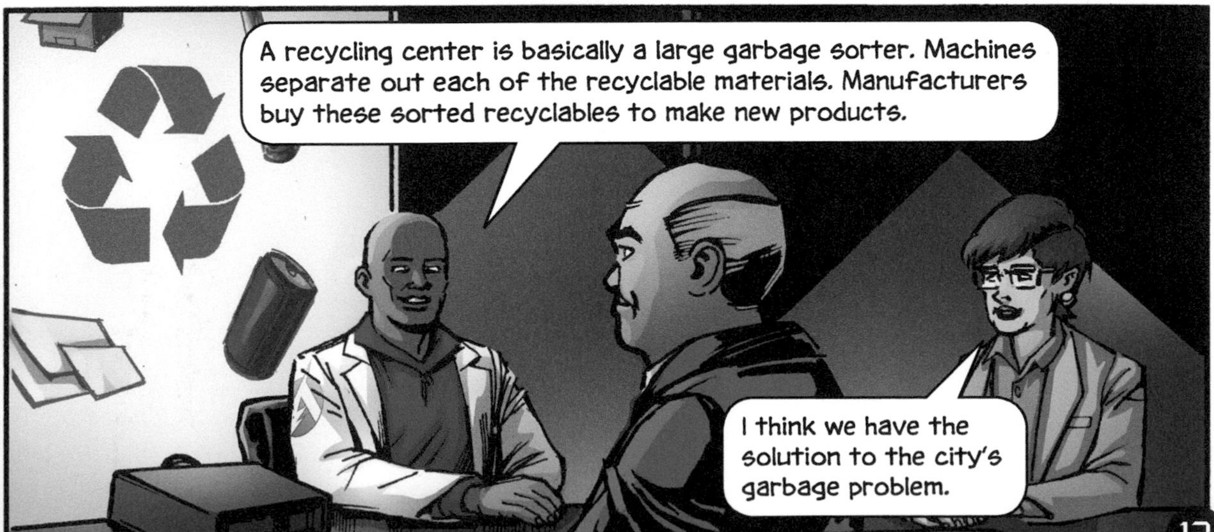
A recycling center is basically a large garbage sorter. Machines separate out each of the recyclable materials. Manufacturers buy these sorted recyclables to make new products.
I think we have the solution to the city's garbage problem.

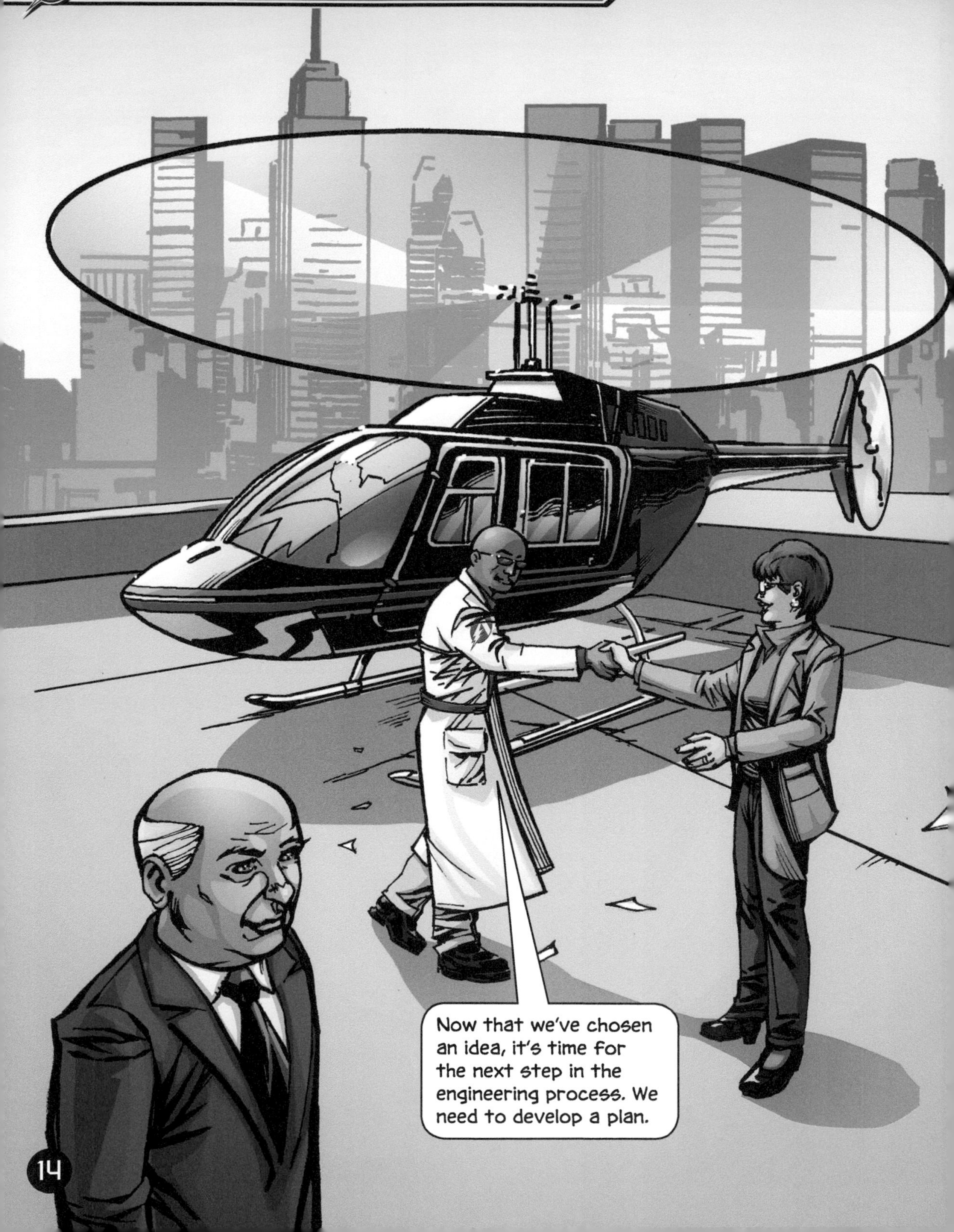
Now that we've chosen an idea, it's time for the next step in the engineering process. We need to develop a plan.

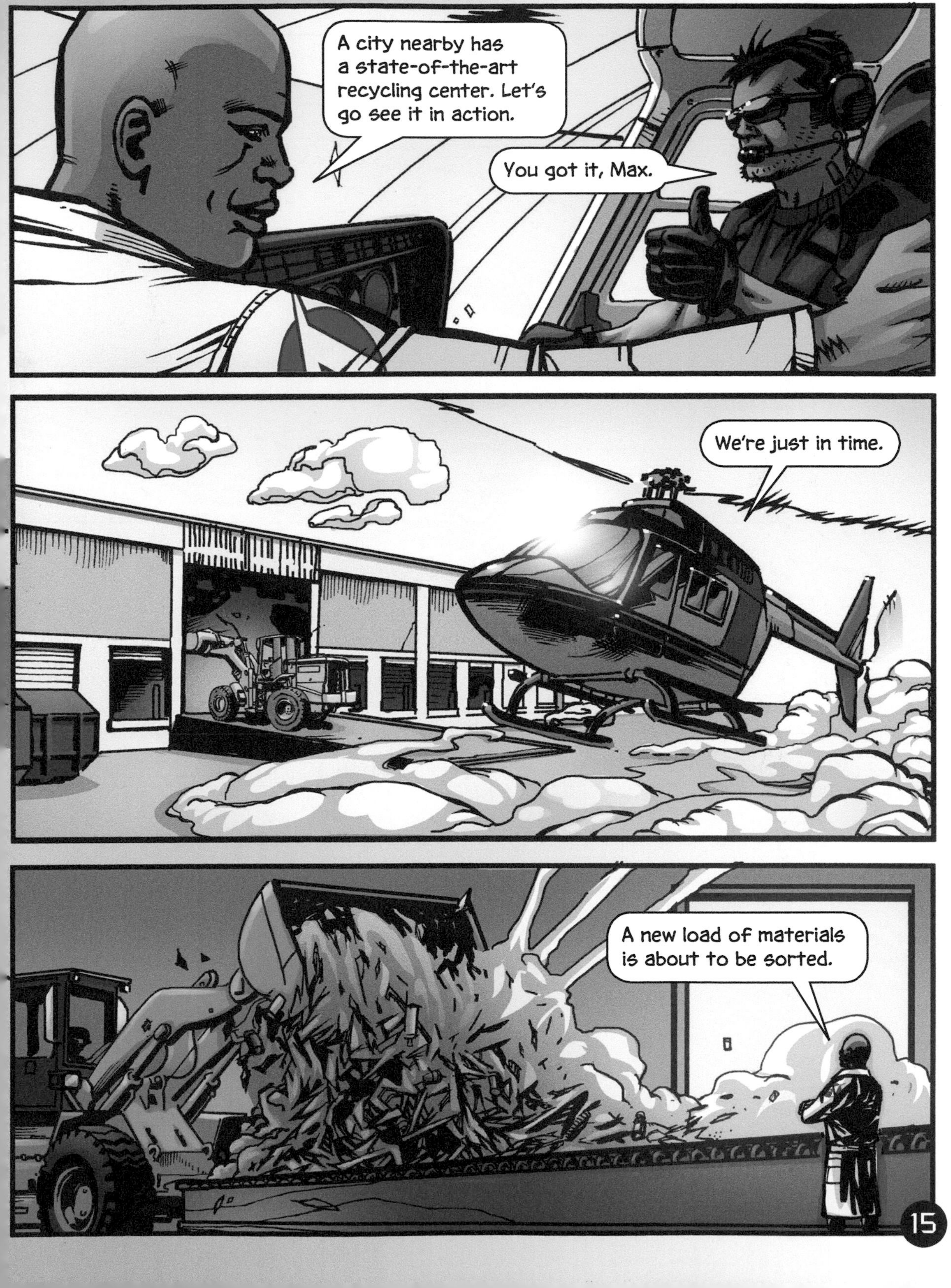
A city nearby has a state-of-the-art recycling center. Let's go see it in action.
You got it, Max.
We're just in time.
A new load of materials is about to be sorted.

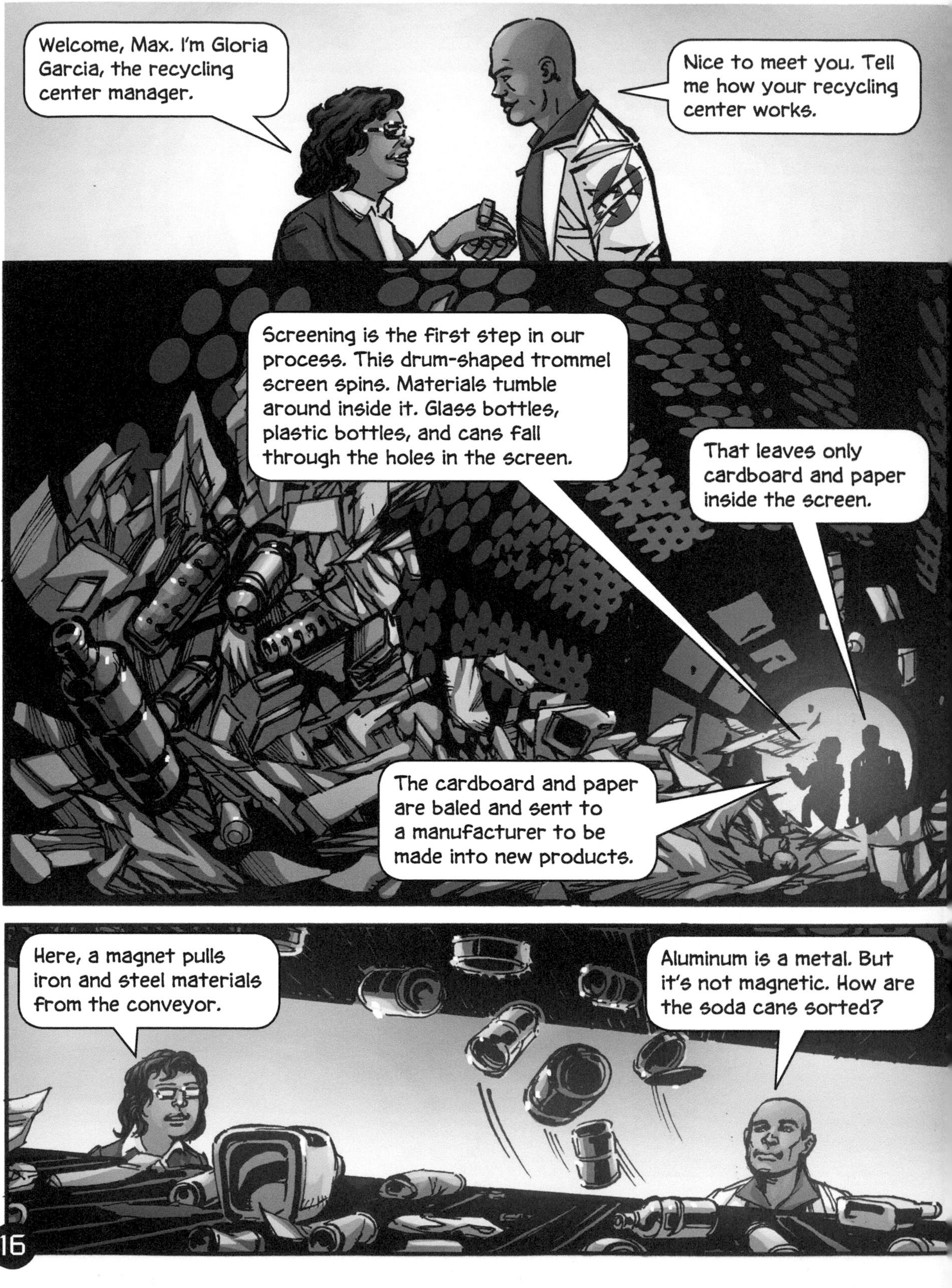
Welcome, Max. I'm Gloria Garcia, the recycling center manager.
Nice to meet you. Tell me how your recycling center works.
Screening is the first step in our process. This drum-shaped trommel screen spins. Materials tumble around inside it. Glass bottles, plastic bottles, and cans fall through the holes in the screen.
That leaves only cardboard and paper inside the screen.
The cardboard and paper are baled and sent to a manufacturer to be made into new products.
Here, a magnet pulls iron and steel materials from the conveyor.
Aluminum is a metal. But it's not magnetic. How are the soda cans sorted?

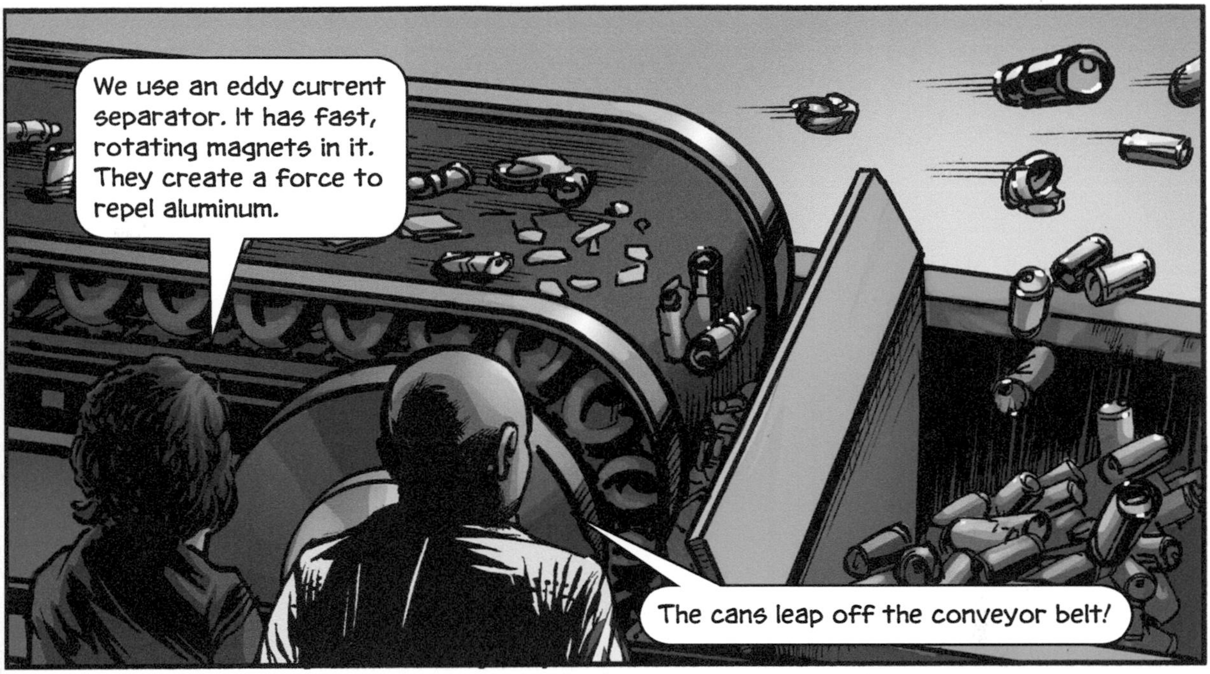
We use an eddy current separator. It has fast, rotating magnets in it. They create a force to repel aluminum.
The cans leap off the conveyor belt!

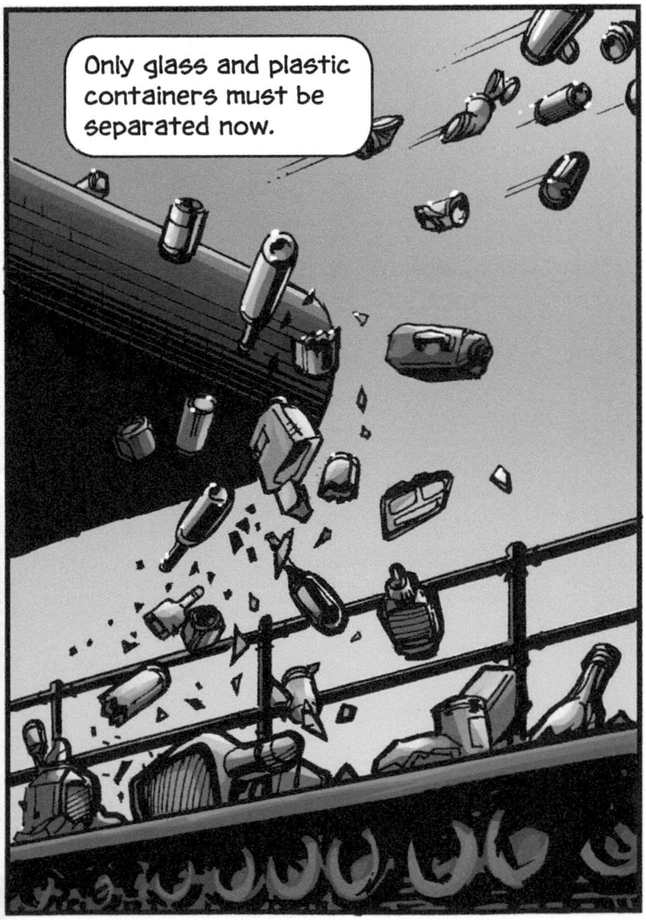
Only glass and plastic containers must be separated now.

Resin Identification Codes

Look at the bottom of a plastic container. The number inside a triangle of arrows is a resin identification code (RIC). The RIC stands for the type of plastic used to make the container. Number 1 stands for polyethylene terephthalate (PET), a plastic used in water bottles and peanut butter jars. Number 2 stands for high density polytheylene (HDPE), which is used in detergent bottles and milk jugs. Although the triangle looks like a recycling symbol, not all plastics with RICs can be recycled. Check with your local recycler to see which numbers are accepted.

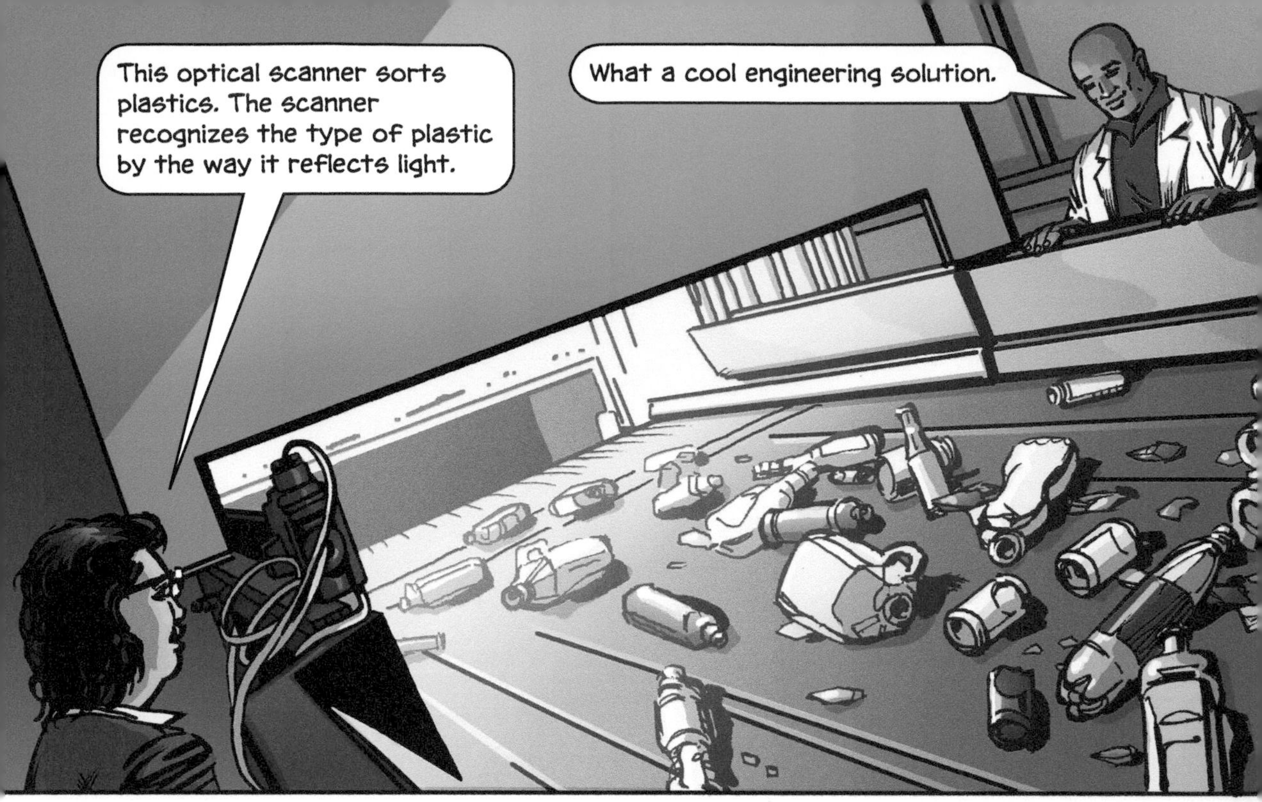
This optical scanner sorts plastics. The scanner recognizes the type of plastic by the way it reflects light.
What a cool engineering solution.

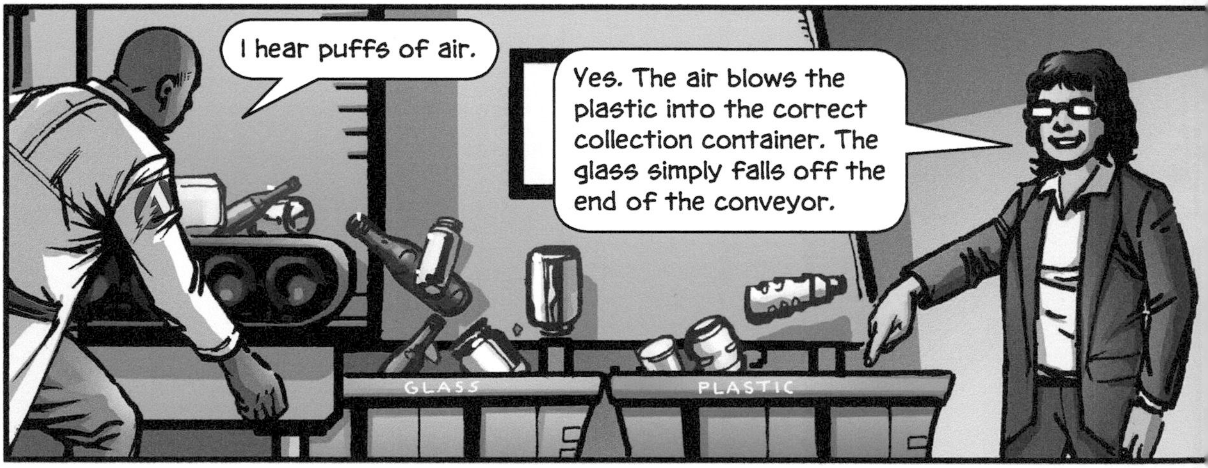
I hear puffs of air.
Yes. The air blows the plastic into the correct collection container. The glass simply falls off the end of the conveyor.
GLASS
PLASTIC

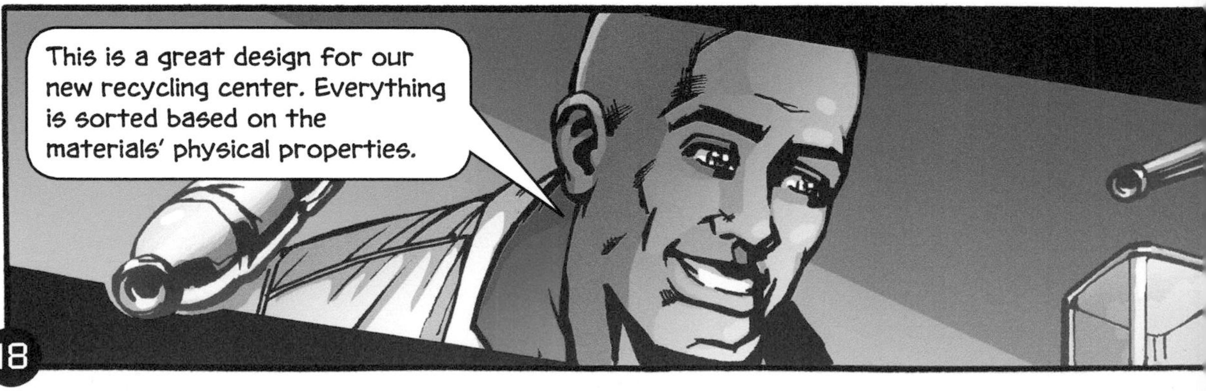
This is a great design for our new recycling center. Everything is sorted based on the materials' physical properties.

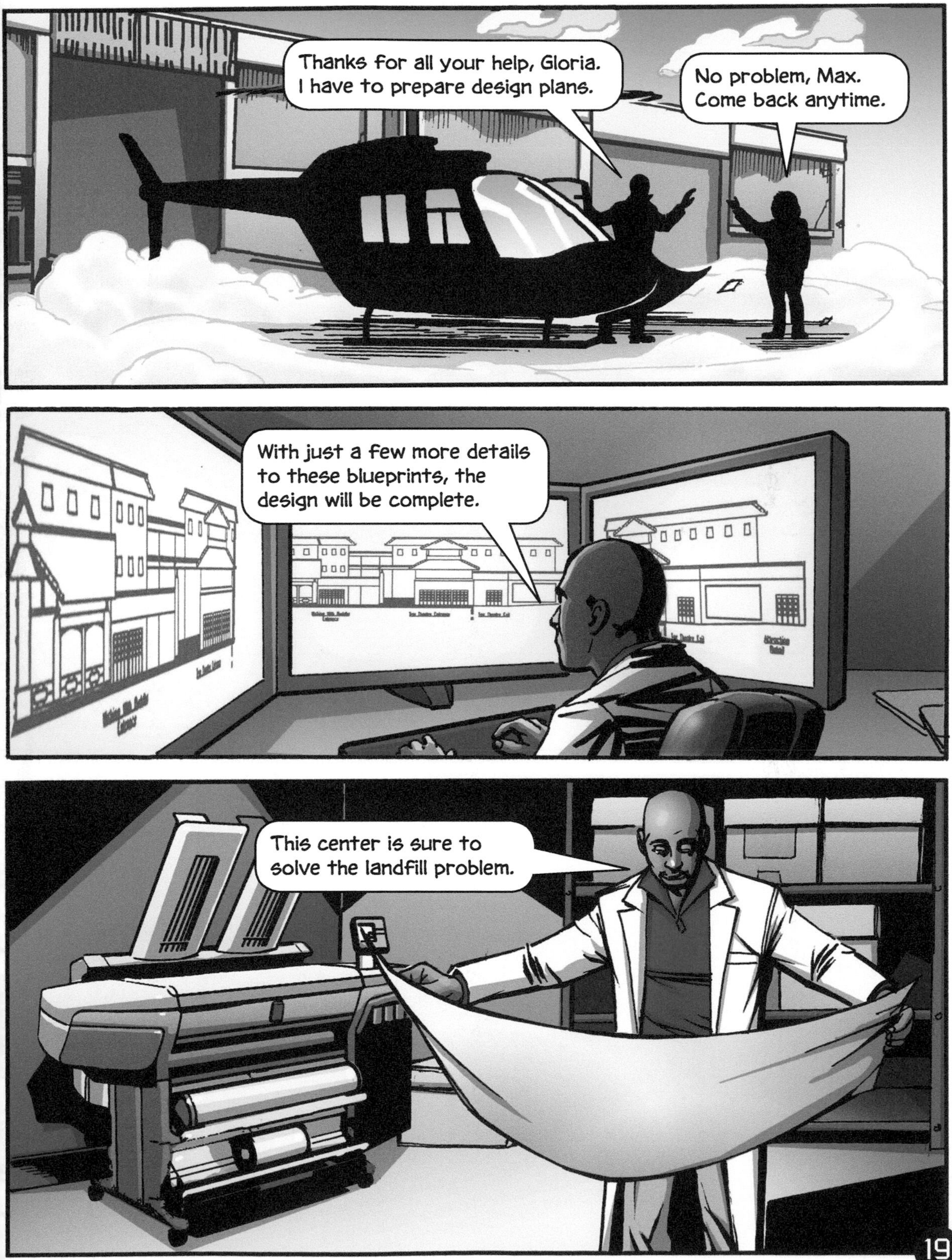
Thanks for all your help, Gloria. I have to prepare design plans.
No problem, Max. Come back anytime.
With just a few more details to these blueprints, the design will be complete.
This center is sure to solve the landfill problem.

SECTION 4
BUILDING A RECYCLING CENTER

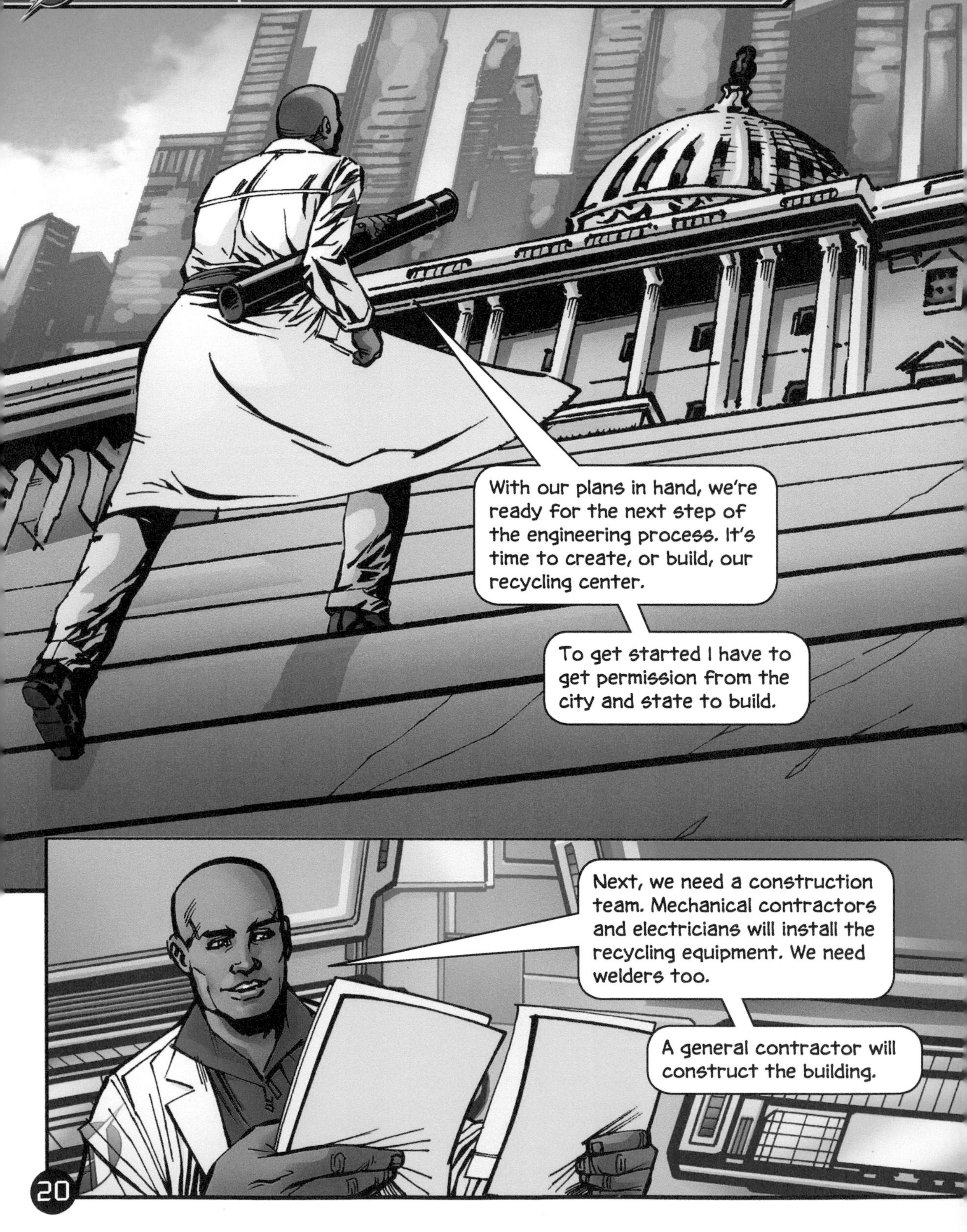

With our plans in hand, we're ready for the next step of the engineering process. It's time to create, or build, our recycling center.
To get started I have to get permission from the city and state to build.
Next, we need a construction team. Mechanical contractors and electricians will install the recycling equipment. We need welders too.
A general contractor will construct the building.

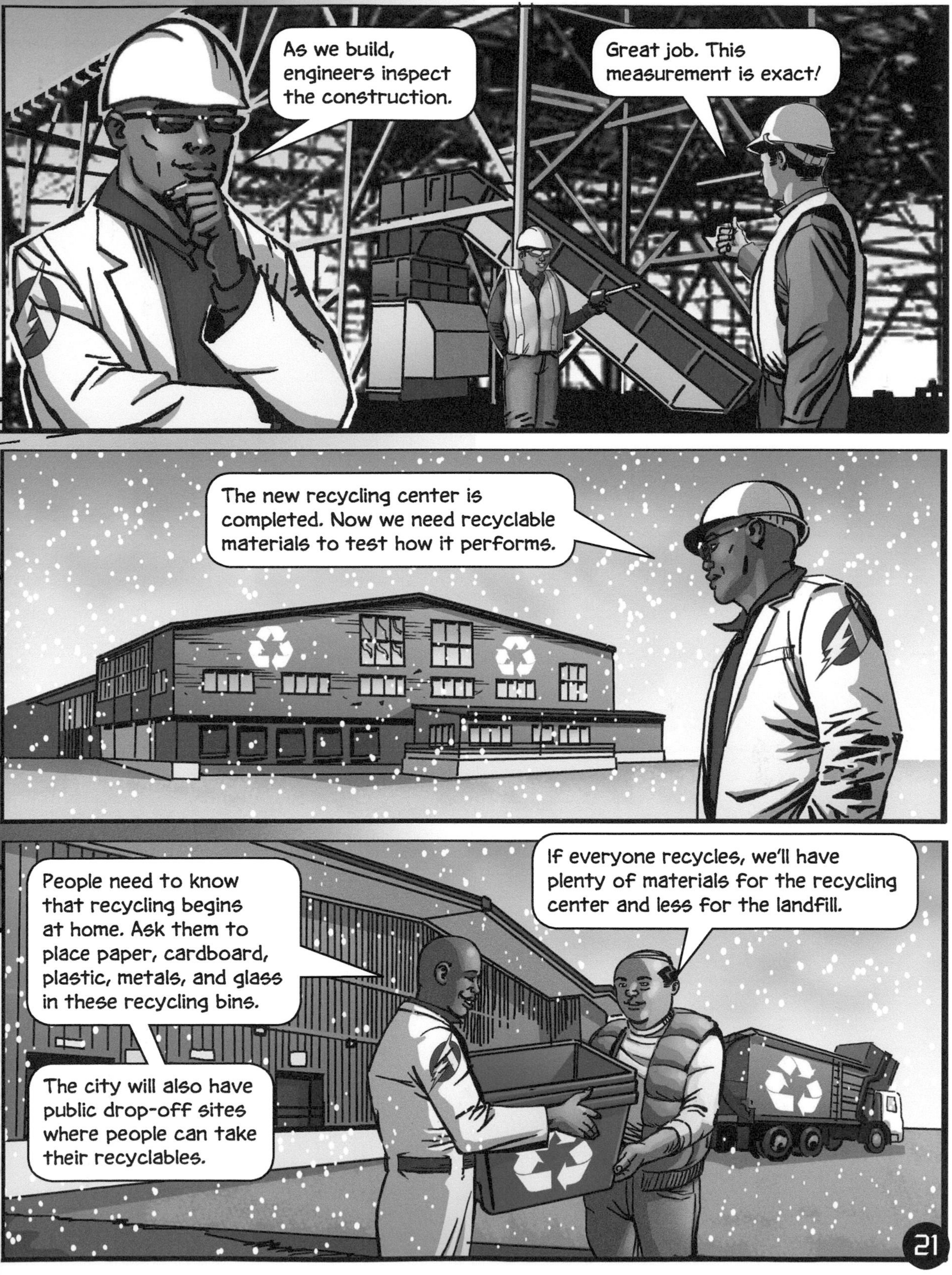
As we build, engineers inspect the construction.
Great job. This measurement is exact!
The new recycling center is completed. Now we need recyclable materials to test how it performs.
People need to know that recycling begins at home. Ask them to place paper, cardboard, plastic, metals, and glass in these recycling bins.
The city will also have public drop-off sites where people can take their recyclables.
If everyone recycles, we'll have plenty of materials for the recycling center and less for the landfill.

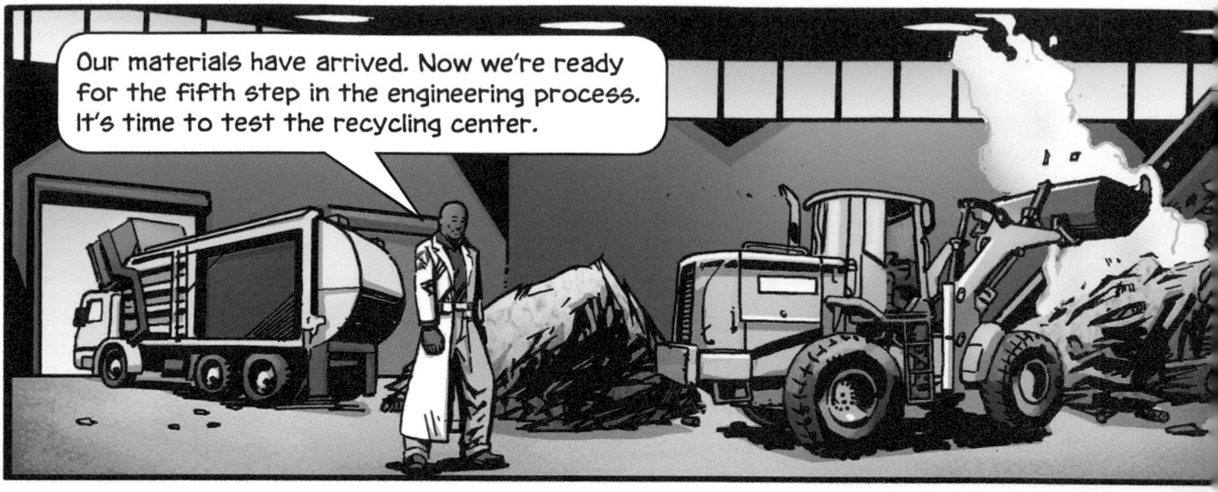
Our materials have arrived. Now we're ready for the fifth step in the engineering process. It's time to test the recycling center.

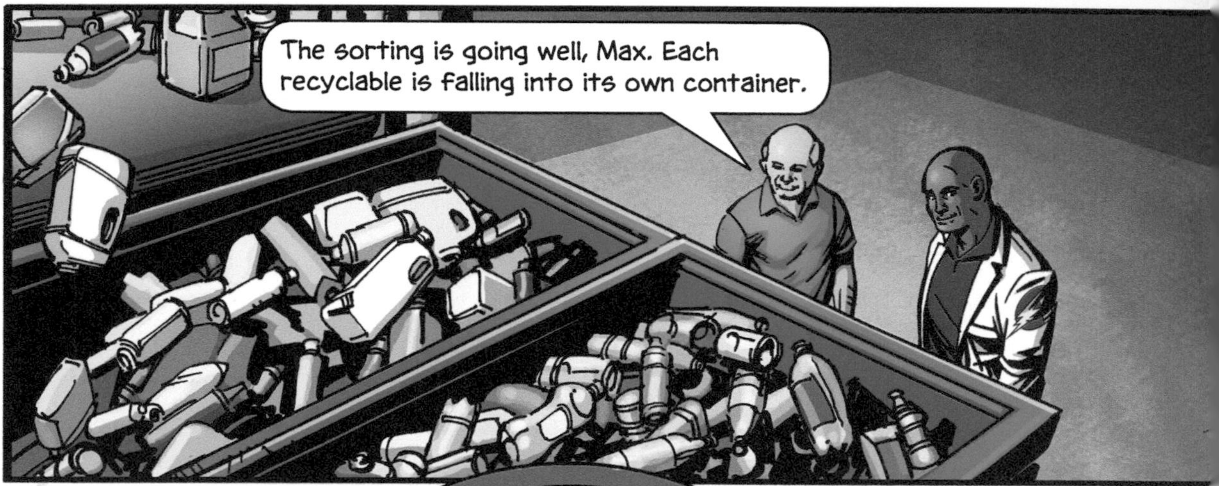
The sorting is going well, Max. Each recyclable is falling into its own container.

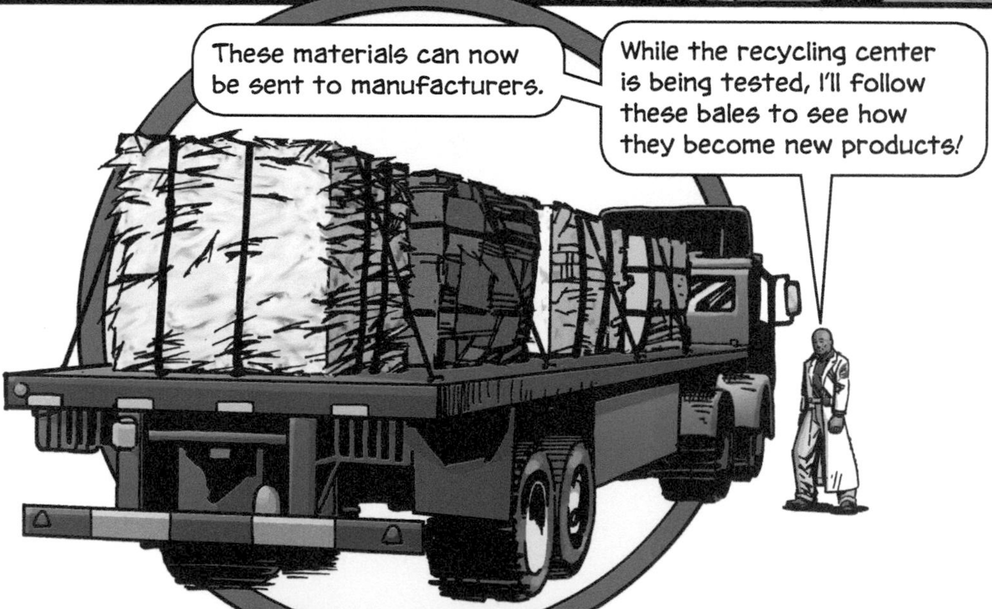
These materials can now be sent to manufacturers.
While the recycling center is being tested, I'll follow these bales to see how they become new products!

At a paper mill, paper and water are mixed and blended to make a slurry. The slurry is washed, screened, and made into new paper products by machines engineers designed.

Metals are shredded at a metal smelter. Then they are melted and made into metal bars. These bars are made into new metal products.

At a glass reclaimer, glass is crushed and mixed with sand, a powder called soda ash, and limestone. Then, it is melted and shaped into new glass materials.

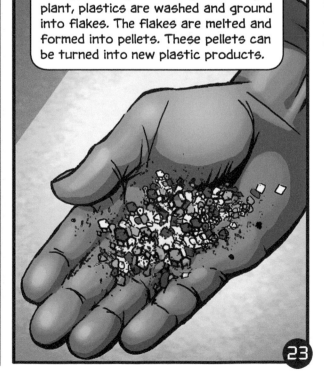

Finally, at the plastics reprocessing plant, plastics are washed and ground into flakes. The flakes are melted and formed into pellets. These pellets can be turned into new plastic products.

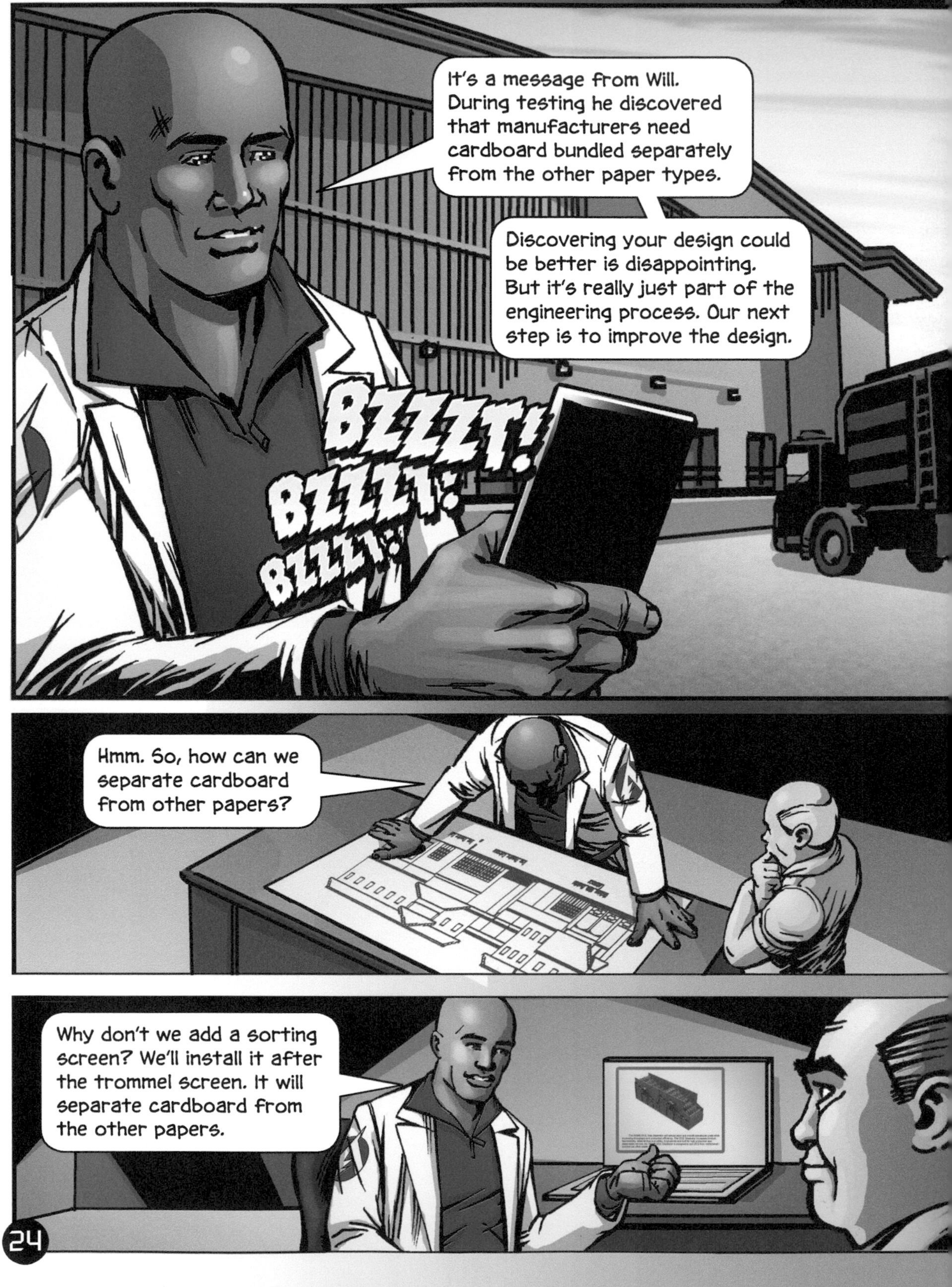
It's a message from Will. During testing he discovered that manufacturers need cardboard bundled separately from the other paper types.
Discovering your design could be better is disappointing. But it's really just part of the engineering process. Our next step is to improve the design.
BZZZZT!
BZZZZT!
BZZZZT!
Hmm. So, how can we separate cardboard from other papers?
Why don't we add a sorting screen? We'll install it after the trommel screen. It will separate cardboard from the other papers.

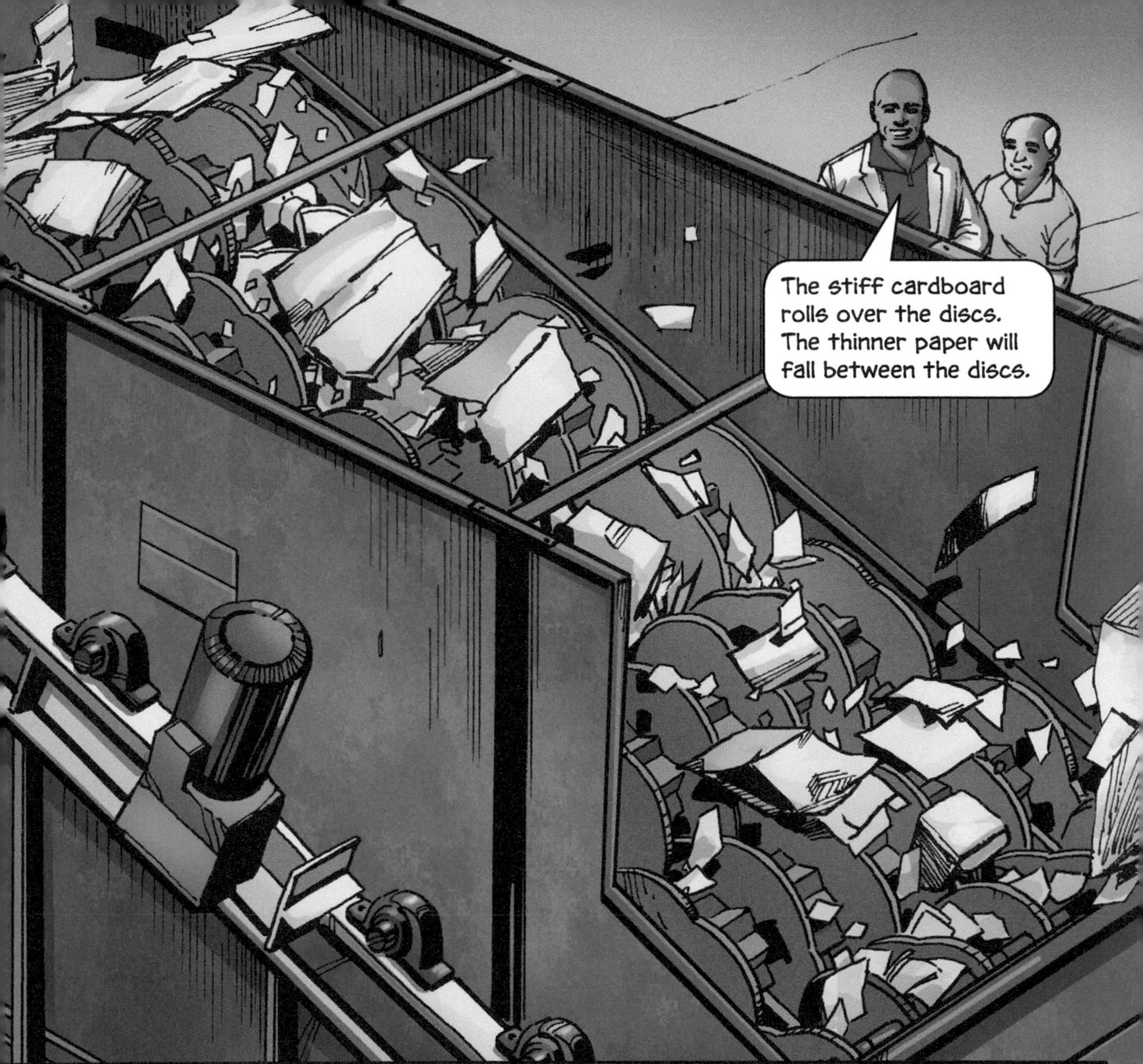
The stiff cardboard rolls over the discs. The thinner paper will fall between the discs.

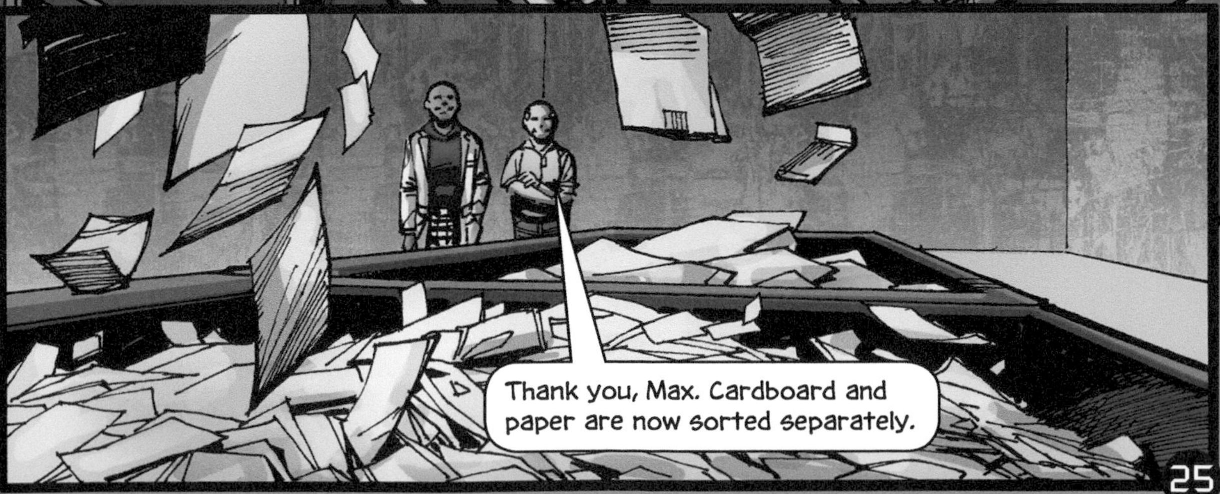
Thank you, Max. Cardboard and paper are now sorted separately.

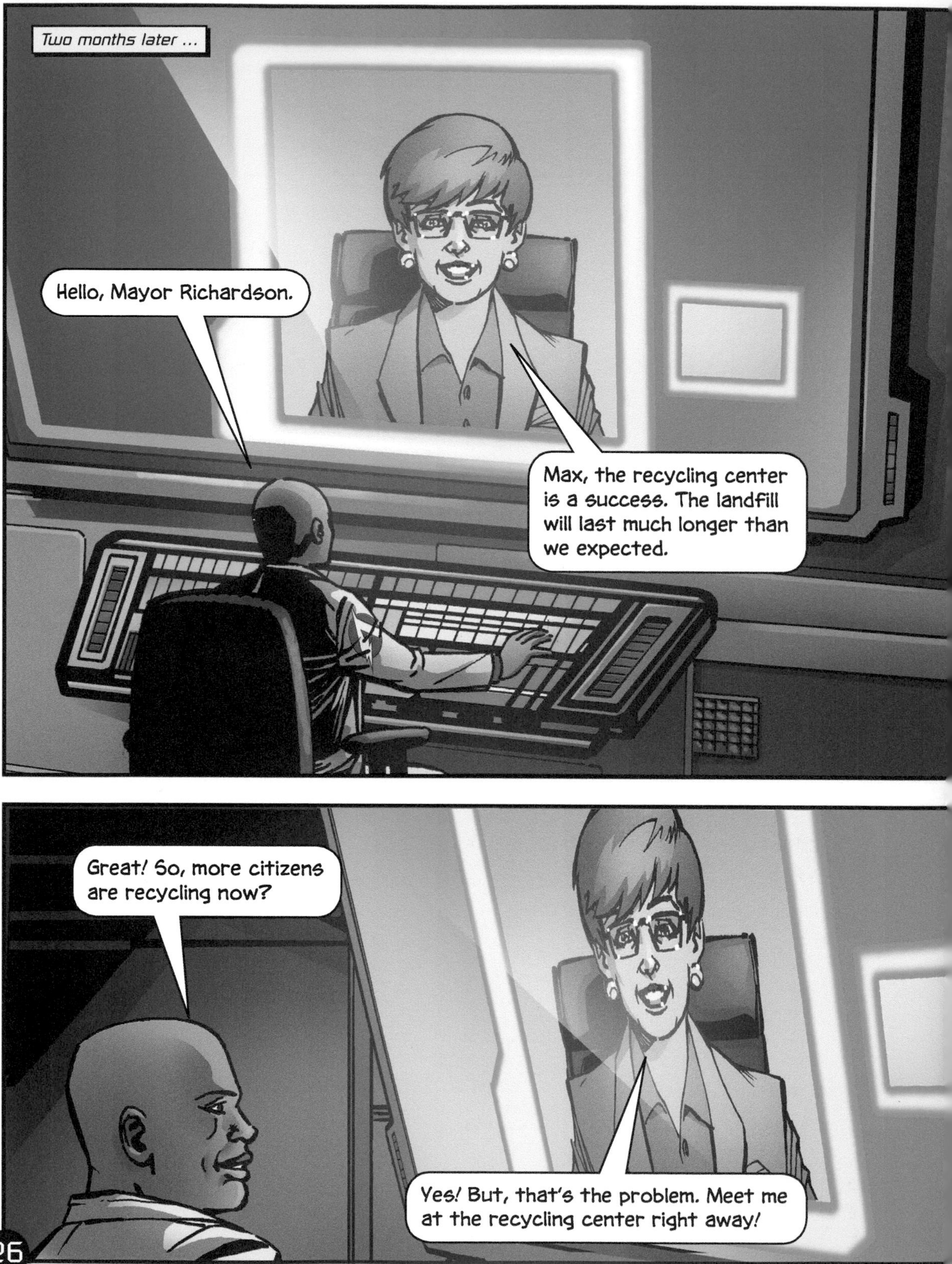
Two months later ...
Hello, Mayor Richardson.
Max, the recycling center is a success. The landfill will last much longer than we expected.
Great! So, more citizens are recycling now?
Yes! But, that's the problem. Meet me at the recycling center right away!

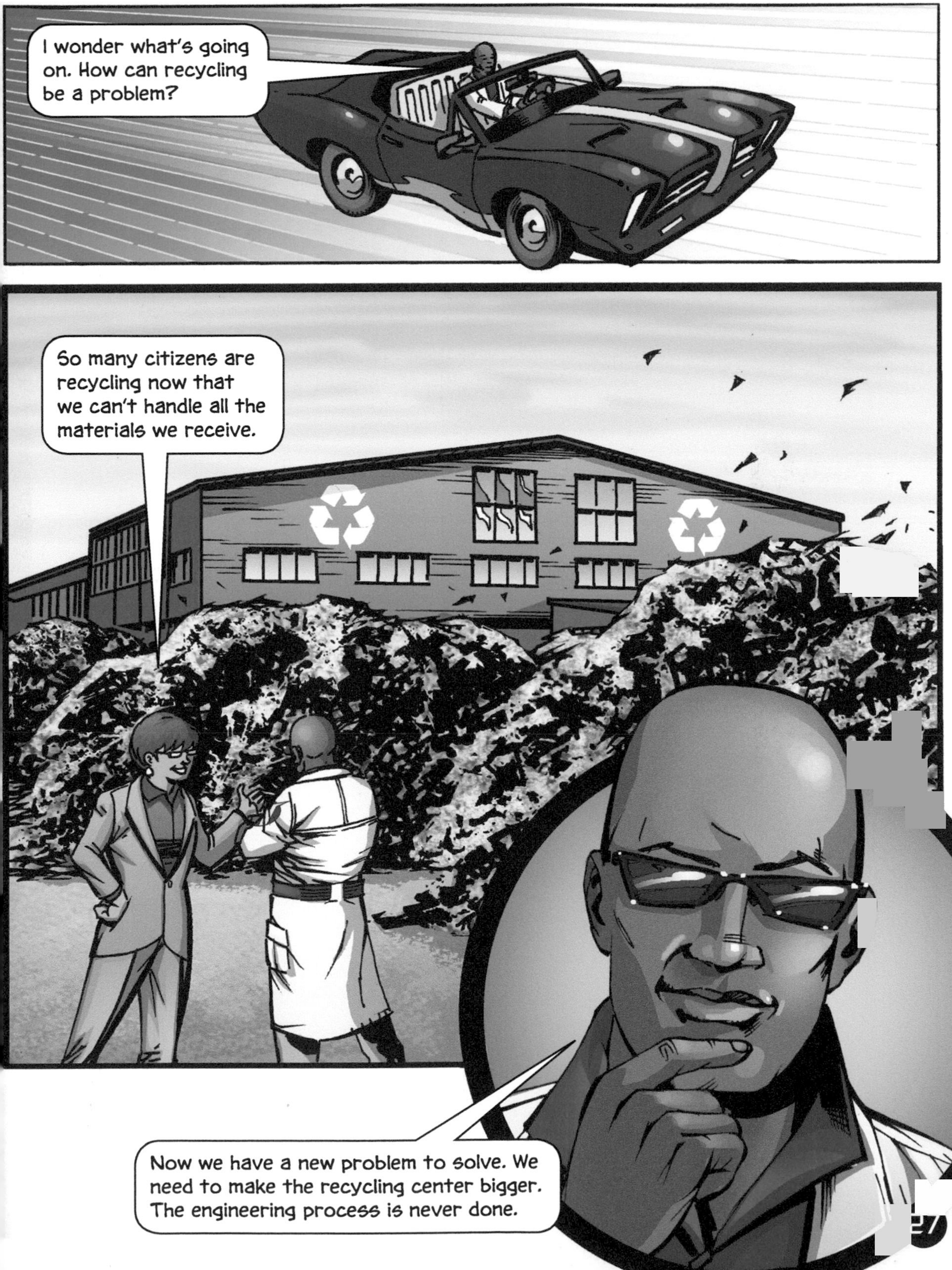
I wonder what's going on. How can recycling be a problem?
So many citizens are recycling now that we can't handle all the materials we receive.
Now we have a new problem to solve. We need to make the recycling center bigger. The engineering process is never done.

RECYCLING AND ENGINEERING

In 2010 the average American created about 4.43 pounds (2 kilograms) of trash each day. Added up, 250 tons (227 metric tons) of trash were created that year. But not all of that trash went to a landfill. Thirty-four percent, or 85 tons (77 metric tons), was recycled or composted.

Engineers and scientists have found ways to use recycled materials to build roadways. Rubber from old tires is ground and blended with asphalt to build highways. Glassphalt is the name given to asphalt that uses crushed glass. Glassphalt roads often shimmer when hit by headlights.

Materials engineers have developed a building material from recycled plastic bottles and other waste plastics. This material was used to build a bridge in Scotland. The bridge is 90 feet (27.4 meters) long, 12 feet (3.7 m) wide, and crosses the River Tweed. Recycling the plastic materials kept 50 tons (45.4 metric tons) of plastic from going into a landfill. In addition, the new bridge won't rust or need paint.

Solid waste engineers have an important job when designing landfills. They stop solid waste in the landfill from polluting soil and water. Engineers build landfills away from sensitive places such as lakes, marshes, and areas that flood. Engineers design liners to keep harmful liquids from flowing out of the landfill. Pump and piping systems are designed to remove harmful liquids from the landfill. Engineers design monitoring wells that make sure that groundwater hasn't been polluted. Engineers also design drainage systems to allow storm water to flow away from the landfill.

Treatment of wastewater, or sewage, is a modern engineering marvel. Engineers design large systems of underground pipes that carry wastewater away from homes and businesses. It is sent to wastewater treatment plants where it is cleaned. Engineers design different steps to clean the wastewater. Larger solids are removed by screening. Settling tanks and skimmer devices remove materials that sink or float. Small organisms are used to eat the waste materials. Chemicals kill any remaining harmful materials before the water is released back into lakes, rivers, or groundwater.

MORE ABOUT

SUPER SCIENTIST

Real name: Maxwell J. Axiom
Hometown: Seattle, Washington
Height: 6' 1" **Weight:** 192 lbs
Eyes: Brown **Hair:** None

Super capabilities: Super intelligence; able to shrink to the size of an atom; sunglasses give x-ray vision; lab coat allows for travel through time and space.

Origin: Since birth, Max Axiom seemed destined for greatness. His mother, a marine biologist, taught her son about the mysteries of the sea. His father, a nuclear physicist and volunteer park ranger, schooled Max on the wonders of earth and sky.

One day on a wilderness hike, a megacharged lightning bolt struck Max with blinding fury. When he awoke, Max discovered a newfound energy and set out to learn as much about science as possible. He traveled the globe earning degrees in every aspect of the field. Upon his return, he was ready to share his knowledge and new identity with the world. He had become Max Axiom, Super Scientist.

GLOSSARY

asphalt (AS-fawlt)—a black tar that is mixed with sand and gravel to make paved roads

blueprint (BLOO-print)—a diagram that shows how to construct a building or other project

compost (KOM-pohst)—to make vegetable matter or manure into soil

density (DEN-si-tee)—the amount of mass an object or substance has based on a unit of volume

eddy current separator (E-dee KUR-uhnt SEP-uh-rate-ur)—a machine that uses a strong, circular magnetic field to separate metals from non-metals

incinerator (in-SIN-uh-ray-tur)—a furnace for burning garbage and other waste materials

optical scanner (OP-tuh-kuhl SKAN-ur)—a machine that uses a light beam to recognize text, images, or materials

organism (OR-guh-niz-uhm)—a living thing such as a plant, animal, bacterium, or fungus

recyclables (ree-SYE-kluh-buhls)—things that can be used again

resin (REZ-in)—a semisolid substance that is made when oil and gas are refined; the resin is used to make plastics

screen (SKREEN)—to separate materials by size on a surface containing openings

slurry (SLUR-ee)—a semiliquid mixture of paper and water

smelter (SMELT-ur)—a factory for melting metal

READ MORE

Enz, Tammy. *Repurpose It: Invent New Uses for Old Stuff.* Invent It. Mankato, Minn.: Capstone Press, 2012.

Green, Jen. *Garbage and Litter.* Reduce, Reuse, Recycle! New York: PowerKids Press, 2010.

Orme, Helen. *Garbage and Recycling.* Earth in Danger. New York: Bearport Pub., 2009.

Rodger, Ellen. *Recycling Waste.* Saving Our World. Tarrytown, N.Y.: Marshall Cavendish Benchmark, 2009.

Silverman, Buffy. *Recycling: Reducing Waste.* Do It Yourself. Chicago: Heinemann Library, 2008.

INTERNET SITES

FactHound offers a safe, fun way to find Internet sites related to this book. All sites on FactHound have been researched by our staff.

Here's all you do:

Visit *www.facthound.com*

Type in this code: 9781429699341

 Check out projects, games and lots more at
www.capstonekids.com

INDEX

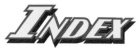